Wrestling
with God

Also by Steve R. Bierly

Help for the Small-Church Pastor
How to Thrive as a Small-Church Pastor

Wrestling with God

A No-Holds-Barred Approach to Knowing God

steve r. bierly

GRAND RAPIDS, MICHIGAN 49530 USA

ZONDERVAN™

Wrestling with God
Copyright © 2003 by Steve R. Bierly

Requests for information should be addressed to:
Zondervan, *Grand Rapids, Michigan 49530*

Library of Congress Cataloging-in-Publication Data

Bierly, Steve R., 1955-
    Wrestling with God : a no-holds-barred approach to knowing God /
    Steve R. Bierly.
       p. cm.
    ISBN 0-310-24778-0
    1. Spiritual life—Christianity.   2. Spiritual life—Biblical teaching.
    I. Title.
    BV4509.B54 2003
    248.4—dc21

                                         2003008388

Interior design by Susan Ambs

Printed in the United States of America

---

03 04 05 06 07 08 09 /❖ DC/ 10 9 8 7 6 5 4 3 2 1

Dedicated to my wife and my parents

and

George and Barb Stanton and Katie and Dale Van Veldhuizen,

wrestlers all

and

Verlyn Boone, colleague and friend

and

The What Four and The Decades (especially Don and Aaron

Mohr, Terry Watson, Al Skutt, Doug Magee, and Tom Applin).

Rock on!!!!

Contents

Acknowledgments

Thanks to my editors—my wife and Jim Ruark at Zondervan—who encouraged me to make this a better book than it otherwise would have been.

The stories in this book are true, or are composites of true stories. The names have been changed to protect the innocent, and the guilty, too, for that matter!

Part One:

What Is It, and Do I Have to Do It?

Chapter 1

In the Beginning Was the Word, and the Word Was Weird!

You don't have to read very far in the book of Genesis before you run across some very strange things—"sons of God" and "daughters of men" joining together to have children who grew to become giants (Genesis 6:1–4), a form of animal husbandry that included placing peeled branches in front of mating goats so that they would bear "streaked or speckled or spotted" young (Genesis 30:25–43), and the story found in Genesis 32:22–32 of Jacob wrestling with a man who seemed to be God, and winning.

What are we to make of this account of a mere mortal fighting with God? Is this only another tale to make us scratch our heads in wonder over an ancient culture that we can't possibly hope to understand fully? Is it just something to give the seminary professors and pastors a mystery to argue over and write papers and articles about?

As I heard the story in Sunday school while I was growing up, I put it in the "really weird" category. Because I liked to read about unexplained phenomenon, UFOs, haunted houses, Big Foot, and such, the story made quite an impression on me. Every time I heard it, I used to wonder what it would be like to have a strange celestial being suddenly appear before me and start to grapple with me. Then, in my bedroom on cold upstate New York winter nights, when the wind howled through the trees, I would fervently hope and pray that whatever strange beings were out there in the cosmos wouldn't notice that I had been wondering about such things and would leave me alone. And that they would quit hiding in my closet waiting to ambush me after my parents went to bed and were asleep.

However, the older I got, and the older I still get, the more I have come to see that I have often wrestled with the same being that Jacob and others in the Bible struggled with. I know what it's like to get into the ring with God. Genesis 32 is not just relating something that happened a long, long time ago in a galaxy far, far away. It's telling my story. And yours as well. In fact, it and other passages with similar themes in the Bible are describing a condition quite common to believers down through the ages and today.

> The older I get, the more I have come to see that I have often wrestled with the same being that Jacob and others in the Bible struggled with.

Finding it hard to believe me? Then join me as I watch my favorite program on "ESPN" (the Eternal Sports Network), "WWG: Wrestling with God," and see if some of the highlights shown there seem familiar to you, or if you've known people in the same sorts of situations. Ready? Good. I'll turn my spiritual television set on now. Oh, look! There's the announcer, Phil Mykup Lord, wearing his blazer and opening the program with his trademark shout . . .

"Let's Go to the Video Tape!"

"This is Phil Mykup Lord with today's wrestling recap.

"We zoom in first on a mother who has been praying for years that her son would see his need for the Lord, repent, and come to

Christ for salvation, but so far, her persistent prayers have gone unanswered. Still, we see her praying again. And, indeed, we've had her in the highlights every night for as long as I can remember. She just keeps right on praying, even while sometimes asking herself whether it's doing any good.

"Let's cut now to Mary. Mary has had a bad week—no, make that a bad month. Okay, it was a bad year. Her faith is at its lowest ebb, and she often doesn't feel like much of a Christian. And she certainly doesn't ever feel like going to church anymore and sometimes skips the services. But other times, like today, we see her walking through the doors into the sanctuary. She's not really expecting to get all that much out of the service, but somehow she still is hoping deep inside that perhaps God can reach her.

"And now, here's a sad one. Sensitive viewers may need to turn away. John has a terminal illness, and every day he is in great pain. He has no 'quality of life' and can't understand why the Lord is keeping him here on earth. He longs to go on to his heavenly home, but the Lord seems to have those doors securely locked for the moment. Does God enjoy seeing him suffer like this? Is God even there at all? Yet, here are believers visiting with him and praying with him, and suddenly, he finds himself clinging to the old beliefs.

"Then there's Stu. Stu had dedicated his new business to God, even faithfully tithing all his profits and witnessing to his clients about God's love. He claimed the biblical promises that God would honor and bless those who honored him, and he knew that the Lord wanted him to provide for his family and be a light in his community. Yet, the business went under, and Stu was forced to declare bankruptcy. Now we see him on his knees. Every day he asks himself and the Lord *why* things turned out the way they did.

"Through the magic of our ESPN camera, we look in on Pastor Donna. Pastor Donna keeps trying to recapture the joy and expectation she felt when she first entered the ministry, but she was forced out of her previous congregation during a bitter power struggle. Donna feels abandoned by God as a consequence. Still, she takes her place behind the pulpit and proclaims his name on this, and every, Sunday morning in front of her new congregation.

"And here's someone looking both queasy and expectant, if you can believe that! Bill was secure that he knew the truth—that is, until he met Christians from another church who questioned his positions on the end times, spiritual gifts, and Christian social action. He's now throwing himself into studying the Bible and reading good books on the subjects to prove that he's right, though he's discovering that he may very well be wrong. He is both exhilarated by, and a bit fearful of, what he's finding. He works at putting aside concerns about where his quest for truth may lead him and what he may have to do as a result. Instead, he keeps on keeping on, sometimes overjoyed, sometimes totally perplexed. Bill refuses to give in to the temptation to despair of ever finding what he's looking for, and he won't buy the lie that the Bible can mean whatever one wants it to mean. Like agent Mulder on TV's *The X-Files,* Bill knows that 'the truth is out there,' and he's determined to uncover it. Go, Bill, go!

"We pan across town to look in on Linda, who is out on a date. Linda's relationship with Paul broke up despite the fact that she honestly believed that he was the one whom God had given her. Now she's starting to get serious with the new guy she's with, Carl, but finds herself wondering if she can and should trust herself, another man, and, more importantly, God again. But she's eating supper with Carl, nonetheless, and notice that they both started the meal with prayer.

"Next, we look in on a man sinking down into a pew. Every time Ted goes to church, he feels that the preacher is speaking directly to him. He knows God wants him to make some changes in his life, but he's been putting off doing so for quite some time. However, God is wearing him down, just as the Lord wore him down a couple of years ago through the witnessing of friends who systematically removed all of his intellectual objections to the faith until he finally gave up and became a Christian.

"Finally, we see Pastor Steve shaking his head and wiping a tear away from his eye as he turns off his computer."

What? I'm in the highlights? I didn't know they filmed me!

"He has just received another email from back home. Although Pastor Steve is currently serving a church in America's heartland, he was born and raised in the Northeast. Now, you can see that Pastor Steve is no spring chicken . . ."

Hey, watch it, Phil!

" . . . so his relatives, friends, and members of his extended family are also getting up there in years. He misses them terribly. Often this homesickness trans-lates into physical pain. He continually hears about health problems and concerns that are besetting those he loves. He longs to be able to help them and to be with them in their

> God is wearing him down, just as the Lord wore him down a couple of years ago until he finally gave up and became a Christian.

hours of need and to spend time with them while there still is time to spend. Yet, he is miles and miles and miles away. He accepted his current call when, through a series of circumstances, it seemed that God wanted him to. But now he has some serious doubts. Maybe he read God wrong. Not a day goes by without him asking God why he brought him to his present church and what God has in mind for him here beyond just attending to the normal pastoral duties. But as of yet, no grand plans have been revealed. Indeed,

God doesn't seem to be saying all that much. Still, Pastor Steve keeps asking, even though he struggles with the feeling that his prayers are just bouncing back to him off of the clouds, and with a niggling doubt that keeps surfacing in his mind that maybe God doesn't really care and isn't all that involved, after all. He keeps on doing much the same sorts of things that he did in the ministry back East—preaching and teaching the Word, helping people with their problems, and sharing their joyous times and their periods of grief. He hasn't thrown in the towel yet, but he wonders why he couldn't do these same sorts of things in a church closer to home. He even questions the divine logic behind assigning him to help other people through their hard times and to attend other families' weddings, anniversaries, baptisms, birthdays, and funerals, while, half a continent away, pastors who are relative strangers are going to his own family's celebrations and wakes, and helping his loved ones through crises. Still, Pastor Steve holds on to God, knowing that God could give answers and clarity in a moment, if he chose to. Besides, Pastor Steve has nowhere else to turn. He realizes that only Jesus has the words of eternal life and that God is the One and only Sovereign in charge of all things. So he's still a Christian and still a pastor. Confused and grieving at times, to be sure, but a believer and a minister, nonetheless.

"We'll be back after a commercial break and take a look at a classic spiritual wrestling bout—Michael versus the Dragon."

If you don't mind, I . . . I'll turn the television off now. Just let me get a Kleenex and I'll continue. It's just . . . see, I have something in my eye.

I'm okay now. So let me point out that all of the Christians featured on Phil's program, including me, are wrestling with God, whether they realize it or not. And maybe now you have an inkling of what wrestling with God is. I'll explain further.

An Explanation of the Match

For years I had caught snatches of hockey games on TV, but I never was all that interested in the sport. For one thing, I didn't understand some of the rules and penalties. Whistles blew and actions were taken on the rink that made little or no sense to me. I didn't really know what it was I was seeing. But then, while I was in college, I got the chance to go to professional games with friends of mine who were avid fans. They knew the ins and outs

> The spiritual life isn't just chaotic mayhem interrupted by sleep, but also a game of strategy and finesse.

of the rules and were happy to patiently explain the game to me. I grew to appreciate and love the sport, looking forward to our trips to the Rochester War Memorial to see the Americans play. No longer did the game seem to be chaotic mayhem on ice. Er . . . I mean no longer did it seem to be solely chaotic mayhem on ice. (Chaotic mayhem on ice is part of hockey's appeal, it must be admitted.) But it was also a game of strategy and finesse. I could enjoy the good plays, sigh over the bad ones, and loudly second-guess the refs with the rest of the fans.

It is my hope that, through this book, you will come to understand and appreciate what wrestling with God is all about and that you'll see that the spiritual life isn't just chaotic mayhem interrupted by sleep, but that it is also a game of strategy and finesse.

I hope that you'll learn the rules of wrestling and what constitutes a "good move." I want you to grasp how to perform the holds, counter holds, and reversals necessary to score points, and how to avoid fouls and disqualifications. I want you to be able to cheer on those who are exhibiting skill and style in their matches and to be able to knowledgeably coach and correct those who are floundering in the ring.

To this end, let me now give you a simplified explanation of what wrestling with God is, and then I'll elaborate in the following chapters.

Essentially, going to the mat with God entails:

1. *Holding on to God no matter what he seems to be trying to do or allowing to happen in order to shake you off.* The "man" Jacob wrestled with wanted to get away at daybreak, but Jacob said, "I will not let you go unless you bless me" (Genesis 32:26).

2. *Pinning God down and getting answers to your prayers and questions.* Jacob refused to let go, and the man told him that he had struggled with God and that he had overcome. And Jacob got his blessing (Genesis 32:28–29).

3. *At times, getting pinned by God, totally floored by his power and his answers.* God wrenched Jacob's hip and refused to tell Jacob his name, proving to Jacob that he was still the One in control (Genesis 32:25, 29).

Now, in light of the above, I ask you, "Have you ever wrestled with God?" If you have, you'll do so again. If you haven't, you will. Why? Because it is part of the very nature of our relationship with the Lord, as we shall see. And it seems as if God himself wouldn't have it any other way. In the next chapter, we'll explore the question, "Why would a loving, compassionate God want to wrestle with us? Why would he keep us struggling with, and clinging to, him? Why make us wait for answers and practically knock ourselves out to obtain them? Why not just deal with us swiftly and be done with it?"

It's Your Turn!

Here are some questions to stimulate your own thoughts as you interact with this chapter, either by yourself or in a group.

1. One of the several things that may strike us as odd about the story of Jacob wrestling with God is that God comes to Jacob on the night before Jacob has to do a very difficult task, meeting again the brother he had cheated out of his birthright years before. God knew when Jacob needed to find strength and encouragement and chose that precise moment to appear to him. Do you have a hard time with the idea that God would be that personally involved with someone's life? With your life? Why or why not?

2. Are there other portions of the Bible that strike you as being really weird? Have you still been able to get something out of them? Are there parts of the Bible that you never get anything out of? Why do you think they are in there?

3. Does the concept of wrestling with God and the examples I've given seem alien to you? Do you think that you might have wrestled with God at some point and just not realized it?

4. Think back to a time when you were wrestling with God, whether you knew it or not. What was the outcome? Maybe you're wrestling with him right now. What do you think the outcome will be? If you are studying this book with a group, are there some experiences you can share with the others?

5. It's possible for a local congregation as a whole, and even for an entire denomination, to wrestle with God. Has your church or denomination ever done that? If so, what can you recall about that time?

6. Is asking questions a sign of strong faith or weak faith? Could it depend on the person, the circumstances, or the questions? If so, how does one tell the difference between strong and weak faith?

7. Are there any questions or concerns you have after reading this chapter?

Chapter 2

Why God Is a Wrestling Fan

Believe it or not, God likes to see you sweat (at least spiritually). In this chapter, we'll explore why this is so.

Hide-and-Seek

Did you like to play hide-and-seek as a child? Well, God, even though he is "The Supreme Adult," likes to play it, too.

The gods of the ancient myths often came down to earth incognito and interacted with humans without the mortals being aware of who they were. They would sometimes drop little hints as to their divine identities. They would speak in riddles and send people on mysterious missions or give them tasks to accomplish. What if these myths aren't just made-up stories? What if, somehow, they captured a bit of the truth about the way the true God deals with us?

Our God is a God who reveals himself, yes, or else why would he have bothered to give us the Bible? But he's a God who often conceals himself, as well. He wrestled Jacob in the dark of the night and wanted to escape before daybreak when the light would reveal his features. Though he did indirectly reveal his identity to Jacob, he still obviously wanted to keep some aspects of himself hidden. When Jacob asks God, "Please tell me your name," the divine being's response is, "Why do you ask my name?" In other words, "I'm not going to tell you." And God remains throughout the Bible as he is in Genesis 32, "the revealed, yet still mysterious" One.

Remember the story of Elijah and how God told him to go stand on the mountain in the presence of the Lord as the Lord passed by? First came a great and powerful wind that shattered even the rocks. But the Lord wasn't in the wind. Then there was an earthquake but still no Lord. Then a fire, but the Lord wasn't in it either. Finally, Elijah heard a gentle whisper: That was the Lord.

Elijah's story, 1 Kings 19:11–13, reminds me of playing hide-and-seek at night with my cousins when I was young. As we got a little older, we all would strain our brains to come up with unusual, unexpected places to hide. We tried to make "It" search awhile to find us. "It" would often first check behind the tree by Grandma's porch. Nope, nobody there. Too predictable! How about in back of the garage? No. Too easy. In the smokehouse? Uh-uh. But wait! Was there some movement way out there in Grandma's garden? Was someone in dark clothes crawling on top of the newly turned-over ground? Would someone really be lying on the cold, wet earth? It's impossible! But that shadow doesn't look quite right. Hey, since when do shadows sneeze? Aha! Gotcha! Elijah, like some of the more inexperienced "Its" who joined us from time to time, looked first for his hidden Lord in the obvious places—in awesome displays of divine power, but God was more subtle than that.

The Old Testament recounts another story that is the mirror image of Elijah's. In Elijah's story, God shows up where he's least expected, but in another book of the Bible, God doesn't show up when we would most expect him to. In Deuteronomy 31 and 32,

God warns the people of Israel that, if they forsake him and worship idols, he will hide his face from them. In other words, if you sin, you can't expect to have fellowship with God. Conversely, if one obeyed God's Law, one would be blessed and protected by the Lord (Deuteronomy 28:1–14). However, the Bible gives us an example of someone who was righteous and dedicated to the Lord, yet who had God's protection and presence removed from him! That man was Job. The Lord let Satan take away Job's wealth, his family, and, finally, his health. And when Job prayed to God,

> In Elijah's story, God shows up where he's least expected, but in another book of the Bible, God doesn't show up when we would most expect him to.

the Bible tells us that the Lord took his time answering Job's cries for help, answers, and justice. God purposely hid his face from righteous Job and, as a consequence, Job felt completely cut off from God. God concealed himself from an upright man who was in desperate need!

The psalmist asked, "Why, O LORD, do you stand far off? Why do you hide yourself in times of trouble?" (Psalm 10:1). And in Psalm 13:1–2 we read, "How long, O LORD? Will you forget me forever? How long will you hide your face from me? How long must I wrestle with my thoughts and every day have sorrow in my heart? How long will my enemy triumph over me?" Doesn't sound as though God was real accessible to him, does it? "Come out, come out, wherever you are!"

At this point, you may be saying, "Yes, but you're quoting the Old Testament. Back in the days it was written, God's full revelation in Christ hadn't yet been given. Much of the truth about him and his ways was cloaked in secrecy and mystery. We now live in the New Testament era." Well, okay, let's check out the New Testament instead.

Turning first to the Gospels, we find that Jesus came to the world in a way that nobody expected. He wasn't the conquering king who would liberate the Promised Land from Rome that the people had hoped, and searched, and longed for. Christ came "in disguise" as a humble carpenter. And not everybody recognized him for who he was.

In fact, it sometimes seemed as if Jesus didn't want to be recognized or have his sermons understood. Instead of using straight talk, Jesus often obscured his messages. Jesus preferred to speak to the crowds in parables. He did this *not* to use interesting analogies and object lessons to *clarify* spiritual truths for the crowd, but to purposely *hide* what he was really saying from the masses. To those who made the extra effort to seek Jesus out and ask him what in the world he was talking about, Christ taught the words of God (Matthew 13:1–23; Mark 4:33–34).

Luke 24:13–35 shows us that even after his resurrection, Jesus continued to conceal himself. He appeared to two of the disciples on the road to Emmaus "in disguise." Though he taught them while they walked together and answered their questions, he didn't let them know who he was. As they came to the village, Jesus even seemingly pretended that he wanted to leave them behind and keep on going. After they urged him to stay, he broke bread for them and gave thanks. Suddenly, they recognized him. This story reminds me of the way I would play hide-and-seek with my children when they were very young. If they couldn't find me, I'd make a noise, like a cough or a laugh, to let them know where I was. At supper, Jesus "made a noise" for the disciples to let them know where he was—right in front of them! And then, it's interesting to note, he instantly disappeared from their sight again!

When he later appears to the disciples by the Sea of Tiberius while they are fishing, Jesus doesn't call out to their boat, "Ahoy!

It's me, Jesus!" Instead, he seems to play a little game with them (John 21:1–14). John only realizes who he is after the miraculous catch of fish, and light doesn't dawn on some of the disciples until they come ashore. Even then, John adds to his written account these cryptic words, "None of the disciples dared ask him, 'Who are you?' They knew it was the Lord." Well, if they knew, why would they even think about having to ask who he was? Evidently, something about Christ's resurrection body revealed, and yet concealed, him at the same time!

After Jesus' ascension, there's more hide-and-seek going on. In the book of Acts, when Paul preached to the Bereans, Scripture tells us, "Now the Bereans were of more noble character than the Thessalonians, for they received the message with great eagerness and examined the Scripture every day to see if what Paul said was true" (Acts 17:11). The Bereans weren't going to take Paul's word that God was really in his message. No, they diligently searched the Scriptures in order to make sure God was there. And they are highly commended for it. The New Testament urges its readers to test the messages that they thought they were receiving from God. Some would be genuine; others would not.

> God wants us to make the effort to search for him, to figure him out, to fathom his words, to see him even when he is camouflaged in the background.

The Bible ends with a book that purposely hides truth in imagery and political references, some of which have meaning to us, and some we scratch our heads over. Down through the centuries, Christians have puzzled over the book of Revelation. John Calvin wouldn't even write a commentary on it because he couldn't understand it.

So we see from the Bible that it's obvious that God wants us to make the effort to search for him, to figure him out, to fathom his words, to see him even when he is camouflaged in the background. The Bible is full of scriptures that instruct us by command or example to search for wisdom and to seek the Lord (e.g., Psalm 27:4, 8–9; Ecclesiastes 7:25). And there are promises that assure us that those who seek, find, and that he is not far from any of us (e.g., Luke 11:9–10; Acts 17:24–28). God's purpose in hiding is not to "win" the game so that he can pop out and say, "N'yah! N'yah! You couldn't find me! Are you ever stupid!" No, his goal is the same as the goal I had when I played hide-and-seek with my toddlers. He wants to have a meaningful relationship with us.

And relationships require effort and time. They don't usually spring up fully formed in an instant. As I was getting to know my wife-to-be, we kept certain things hidden from each other. But as time went on and we talked and shared during our long walks together, we made discoveries about each other. And as trust grew between us, we revealed more and more about ourselves to each other. After nineteen years, we are still learning how each other thinks. As we take time and make the effort to discover who God is and what he's all about, he will naturally reveal himself to us.

As a pastor, I've seen a pattern displayed in the faith journeys of some people who come to know the Lord. At first, they are caught up with the awesome news that God loves them and sent Christ to save them. It seems as though all of their prayers are being instantly answered. As time goes on and they are exposed to the Bible more and more, they begin to be convicted that they need to start rooting out the sins and wrong ways of thinking in their hearts. It's not long before sanctification becomes the dominant idea in their minds. Still later, they suddenly start seeing opportunities to serve God by serving others all around them. But now, maybe the answers to their prayers aren't coming so quickly and easily. God is teaching them that he is the One in charge and isn't taking orders from them. Apparently, God first let them be overwhelmed by his unfathomable love and then began teaching them how to please him and how to spread his love to others. Finally, he started dealing with the issue of his kingship and other weighty matters. It seems to me that God knew the converts couldn't take all of this in at once, so he gently brought them along at a pace they could understand.

Maybe it's really not so much of a case of God purposefully hiding anything at the beginning as it is a case of God not revealing absolutely everything, so as not to overwhelm the new converts.

> We're willing to go to great lengths to uncover the "God who doesn't seem to be there," because we need him in our lives so much.

Not that God deals with everyone in this manner, but I've seen this transition take place in enough lives to be able to hypothesize that this is one way God works as he continually woos his followers.

And speaking of wooing, in the earthly games between potential lovers, some women play hard to get. Some men do, too! They do this in order to find out just how much their suitor really cares about them. Perhaps God's hiding himself can be construed as his playing hard to get. He doesn't say, "Here I am. I'm yours!" He says, "If you want me, you'll have to pursue me. You'll have to look for me with your whole heart." He may do this to find out how much we really desire him, or maybe, more importantly, since he already knows all things anyway, that *we* will realize how much we desire him. That we will see that we're willing to go to great lengths to uncover the "God who doesn't seem to be there," because we need him in our lives so much. In Proverbs 8:17, the personification of Wisdom, who represents Christ, says, "I love those who love me, and those who seek me find me."

As a teenager, I remember being surprised when an unchurched, relatively shy classmate of mine showed up at our youth group meeting one Sunday night out of the blue and demanded to know why all of us in the room believed in God. She proceeded to tell us that she had never seen him or heard him and asked us if any of us ever had. After listening to our points about how God speaks through his Word and his people, and how he answered our prayers, she shook her head and said, "I'm sorry, but if God wants to prove he's real to me, he will have to write my name in blazing giant letters across the sky. If he's real and he's God, he can make the stars do that, right? Or he can shout at me like he's on a loudspeaker or something. Until that day, I can't believe in him." She left the meeting not having found God. But she was definitely seeking him. Why else would she have come to the meeting and been bold enough to say what she did? Soon, she did encounter God, not in the flashy ways she had prescribed, but through friends, prayer, the Bible, and the divine touch upon her heart and soul. She sought and found.

And it's not just the unchurched and unsaved who have to make the effort to seek out God. We Christians often engage in hide-and-seek with him, too. During one period of my life when I was very confused about my future, and my devotional life was dried up to the point of almost being nonexistent, and I couldn't see God's directing hand any place and didn't feel his love, I decided to read a couple of chapters of the book of Job every day. Ironically, as Job was ranting and wailing that God had distanced himself from him, I saw God leaping out at me from the verses. Hidden in Job's probing, his despair, and his debates with his friends, God was saying to me, "Just because you're going through tough times, Steve, doesn't mean that I don't love you or that you are outside of my will. I'm big enough to handle all of your frustration and anger. There are characters in my Word who are just like you, and if I was with them, I'll be with you. I was behind all that happened to Job, and I'm in control of all that happens to you. And, by the way, my including the book of Job in the Bible proves that I care about philosophy majors like you." (The book deals with stuff philosophy majors love to talk about—why bad things occur, the limitations of human knowledge, how one discovers metaphysical truth, etc.) Job may have felt that God was silently hiding from him, but actually, God was there all the time and was proclaiming his truth. I could see him so clearly.

But what if I hadn't made the effort to seek out the Lord in the Bible? Well, if I had been content to leave God alone, he probably would have left me alone—at least for a while. If I hadn't gone looking for him, he would have been content to remain in his hiding place. And God is *very* patient. Unfortunately, I know this from personal experience, because sometimes all I see are the problems, and I forget that God is hiding behind them. I think that he's abandoned me rather than consider that he's in the room with me, crouched behind the sofa, as it were. I act like a toddler panicking during a game of hide-and-seek because "Daddy's gone!" And so I run around, away from the Bible, away from prayer, away from the church. And God lets me go my own, fruitless way for a time, until, in his compassion, he reaches out to me and draws me back to himself—just in time for our next bout!

> Sometimes all I see are the problems, and I forget that God is hiding behind them.

The Family That Fights Together Stays Together

One of the first things I ask a couple when I do premarital counseling is, "Have you ever had any disagreements or arguments?" The answer I'm looking for is not, "Oh no! We always see eye-to-eye on everything because we're perfect for each other and we're so much in love!" No, I want to hear, "Well, sure, but when arguments happen, we talk everything out and work it through." You see, I'm trying to determine if the man and woman have a real relationship, or if, instead, they are just infatuated with a phony image of their beloved. Do they share their real thoughts and emotions with each other, or do they hide their true selves, playing roles and keeping everything bottled up inside? Do they interact with each other, or merely want to share the same living space together?

Believe it or not, God wants an intimate relationship with us. He doesn't want to be used just as our "get out of hell free" card or as a "bless me" machine. He doesn't want to be a concept that we're enamored with, just an object for some lively theological discussion. He wants to be a Person we communicate with. And God doesn't want us to don our "holy masks" when we come into his presence. He wants honesty. He wants to see our true selves. He certainly has no desire to merely share space with us as we worship in the sanctuary Sunday morning. He longs for meaningful interaction with us.

Not that the Lord needs such interaction because he's desperately lonely or anything of the sort. I remember a well-meaning children's book years ago that began the story of Creation by making the little ones feel sorry for poor God who had nobody to talk to before he made the world. However, the Bible teaches that God is a Trinity, three Persons in One, and that the Father and the Son have perfect love for each other and that the Spirit searches and knows the mind of God. How could such an infinite being be lonely? He has eternal companionship within himself! He is self-sufficient in a way no one else can be. And on top of that, he's surrounded by the angels who praise him, report to him what they see and do, and await his counsel and his orders. Poor, little, lonely God? No! The Lord doesn't *need* to have a relationship with us. The miracle of grace is that he *wants* to have a relationship with us.

Therefore, he likes it when we wrestle with him. He wants us to come to him with our questions and our frustrations, crying on his shoulder or beating on his chest, and tell him that though we're upset with him, we're trying to hang in there anyway.

God demands effort from us because he doesn't want his relationship with us to deteriorate to the point some human relationships have, such as some married couples who, by the time they finally drag themselves into Pastor Steve's counseling room, are only one step away from divorce.

"He never tells me anything!" a wife sobs. "I don't know what he's thinking and feeling." Or a husband says, "She spends all her time with her friends at work. She never wants to be with me. She acts like she's single." As I do some probing, I find out that these are long-standing, deep-seated resentments, hurts, and misunderstandings that have been repressed for so long that it's almost impossible to dig them out and deal with them now. Once upon a time, behavior could have been modified, apologies could have been made, commitment could have been strengthened, but now, barring a miracle, it's too late.

I knew a man who became angry with God because one of his daughters, the churchgoing one, had contracted a debilitating disease. However, instead of climbing into the ring with God and having it out with him, the man cut himself off from the little contact he had with the Lord through God's people and God's Word. His resentment against God built up over the years so that, toward the end of his life, it seemed he couldn't or wouldn't even listen to anyone who tried to talk with him about the Lord. At the mere mention of the word "God" or anything having to do with religion, he would just shut down, or change the subject, or turn red and pontificate against the Almighty. His heart had become rock hard and stone cold as far as God was concerned. Once upon a time, it had been open to the idea of God. But years of bitterness and withdrawal had changed all that. Barring a miracle, he went to his grave still unreconciled to God. I prayed for that miracle and, even now, hope that the Holy Spirit broke through his barriers in the end and brought him into the kingdom because I loved him very much. He was one of the nicest, most intelligent, most interesting men I've ever met and put a lie to the myth that people who hate God are ogres. No, he was far from an ogre. He was just a hurt, lost man. If only he had climbed into the ring with God or stayed on the mat with him until he got his blessing like Jacob!

> God is a wrestling enthusiast because he knows that dealing with conflict leads to healthy relationships.

God is a wrestling enthusiast because he knows that dealing with conflict leads to healthy relationships, and that's what he wants with us. He knows that wrestling leads to eternal life, and that's what he desires for us.

Take Your Medicine

I remember a couple of times I had to literally pin my children down for their own good. When my daughter was born, she was jaundiced and blood tests had to be taken. The lab technician at the small community hospital asked me to keep her legs still while the blood sample was drawn. So I had to hold my brand-new little one while the needle went in and the tears welled up in her eyes. It broke my heart. And during my son's toddler years, he accidentally received a dose of a wrong medicine that could have been poisonous to his young system. We had to rush him to the emergency room, where he was forced to drink a foul charcoal concoction that would absorb the dangerous medication and help flush it through him. The little fellow valiantly tried to choke all the yucky stuff down while crying and repeating what we were telling him, "Doctor says, Doctor says . . ." But there were still moments when I had to make sure he was incapable of swatting, or kicking, away the latest cup in the seemingly endless procession.

God wrestles with us because he knows that sometimes we have to be pinned down for our own good.

What the Lord said to Saul when he appeared to him on the road to Damascus is very interesting. That relentless persecutor of the Christians saw a light from heaven and fell to the ground. A voice asked him, "Saul, Saul, why do you persecute me? It is hard for you to kick against the goads." In other words, the Lord had been sparring with Saul for some time and was winning, but Saul kept trying to fight the truth. The Lord wanted Saul to give up. So God revealed himself to Saul, saying, "I am Jesus, whom you are persecuting." Then he struck Saul blind, gave him a commission, and sent him to a city where a Christian would come and pray for him and heal him. God floored Saul, pinning him so there was no chance of escape or further struggles, in order to save him. (See Acts 9:1–19; 26:9–18.)

I've met many people whose dramatic conversion stories echo Saul's. They were starting to be won over to Christianity but still trying to resist its lure, when, all of a sudden, the Lord did, or revealed, something to them that floored them (either figuratively or literally). They then had no choice but to believe.

Sometimes God strives against the old, sinful natures of us Christians for just so long, and if we try our best not to change, he will decide to floor us—letting the consequences of our sinful actions and habits play out their course, or opening our eyes as to how we are hurting ourselves, others, and the Lord's cause, or permitting a speaker's words to hit us hard right between the eyes. Then we'll finally repent and give up a particular sin or sins, asking God to help us as we strive to change. "When I kept silent, my bones wasted away through my groaning all day long. For day and night your hand was heavy upon me; my strength was sapped as in the heat of summer. Then I acknowledged my sin to you and did not cover up my iniquity. I said, 'I will confess my transgressions to the LORD'—and you forgave the guilt of my sin" (Psalm 32:3–5).

One night at my Christian college, God used my roommate to floor me. I had been complaining about a guy on campus who had hurt some close friends of mine by playing the manipulative, self-glorifying, power games he seemed to enjoy. Having had enough, I shouted, "I know we're supposed to pray for our enemies, but that guy doesn't deserve God's love! He doesn't deserve to go to heaven!" My roommate looked at me and quietly asked, "And I suppose you do?" With just those five little words, God hit me over the head (spiritually speaking, of course) and let me see how arrogant I was being. I was full of the same pride I hated in my antagonist! And it suddenly dawned on me that if I expected God to forgive my sins because of his grace, how could I demand that he withhold his pardon from another sinner like me? That evening I understood a lot about myself and about God in ways I hadn't before.

I wouldn't be a pastor today if God hadn't floored me at various points as I tried to follow other paths. I started out to learn how to be either a disc jockey or a television writer, but I found myself taking classes that weren't fulfilling to me in a school I hated. I thought I had my whole future mapped out, but God pulled the rug out from under me. He had another career plan for me.

I also wouldn't have the family I have today if God hadn't floored me a few times along the way. I had been involved in relationships with women who, in retrospect, were not right for me, but that didn't make our breakups any less painful at the time, or lessen the experience of being floored each time they occurred.

God wrestled me (and floored me) and will wrestle (and maybe floor) you for the same reason he wrestled Jacob—in order to bless us.

A Confession

Having tried to explain why God wants to wrestle with us, I have to admit that I haven't exhausted all the reasons, nor could I. I probably can't even understand them all. God's ways are not our ways, and his thoughts are much higher than our thoughts. (Which means, as the next chapter will show, that it's inevitable that we will find ourselves wrestling with him.)

And he may wrestle with us at times simply because he likes spiritual wrestling and enjoys this way of dealing with us!

It's Your Turn!

Here are some questions to stimulate your own thoughts as you interact with this chapter, either by yourself or in a group.

1. Have there been times in your life when God suddenly came out of hiding and you recognized that he was there?

2. Why doesn't God tell us everything we want to know?

3. What does it mean to have a meaningful relationship with God? How healthy is yours?

4. What does the fact that God doesn't need you, but wants you anyway, mean to you?

5. Has God ever "pinned" or "floored" you? How and why?

6. "God may want to wrestle with us simply because he likes it." What's your reaction to that statement?

7. Are there any questions or concerns you have after reading this chapter?

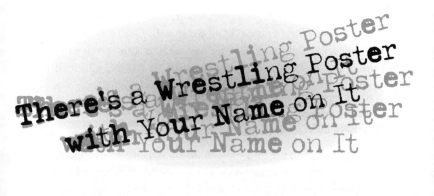

Chapter 3

There's a Wrestling Poster with Your Name on It

Welcome to the Twilight Zone

Here's a plot idea for the old Rod Serling television series:

Picture a wrestler who wants to give up his profession. He's just going to walk away from it all because he's tired, and, frankly, a little scared. He's not as young as he used to be. But just as he's starting to leave the arena, a mysterious stranger who has been hanging around the locker room tells him, "I know what you're trying to do, but it won't work. If you quit now, it will upset the balance of time. You're destined to get into the ring with Muscles McGerk. It's in the cards. It's the very nature of things." The wrestler yells, "You think I can't quit? Just watch me!" and storms out the exit doors. But instead of finding himself in the parking lot, he's suddenly standing on the carpeted path in the arena that leads to the ring. McGerk has already been introduced, and a large crowd is chanting the wrestler's name. Panicked, the old wrestler whirls around and bursts through the exit doors again. But again, he finds himself in the arena on the night of the big match. He slowly comes to the realization that getting in the ring is inevitable. It's the way things are in ... the Twilight Zone!

And in the Christian Zone, too. If you are a believer and serious about working on a relationship with God, it is inevitable that you will wind up in the ring with him at some point in your life, no matter how much you may want, or try, to avoid it. It is simply the way things work, the very nature of reality.

How so? I'm glad you asked.

Holy, Holy, Holy!

If you were to travel abroad among people who were different from you, with unfamiliar languages and cultures, you would have to make a real effort to understand them and what was going on around you.

One doesn't actually have to travel all that far to encounter different cultures even here in America. I moved from a suburb in the Northeastern United States to a small town in Northwest Iowa. One of the first things my wife, my kids, and I found out is that you don't order "soda" here in a restaurant. If you do, the dining area suddenly gets real quiet, and everyone turns their head and stares at you quizzically. You see, out here, it's called "pop." Another thing different is that when an organization or a business in town holds an event—a fund-raiser, a ball game, an open house, etc.—everyone is expected to be there. It's your civic duty to keep the town going by attending all its events. Where we were living before, it was impossible to attend all scheduled events, since many organizations held activities on the same days in the same geographical area. And it was impossible to keep track of who attended what and who didn't.

Another noticeable difference is how people give directions. The first time I asked for directions in Iowa, I was told something like this: "Go north on First Street and then east on Maple for a mile and a half. Then go north again on Oak for two more miles."

I still had no idea of how to get where I wanted to go and had to make a real mental effort to figure out where north and east were. In the Northeast, we were used to, "Turn right at the gas station, then go on First for a ways and take a right on to Maple. Stay on Maple for a mile and a half and hang a left on Oak."

Phrases can also have different meaning in various regions. I can remember asking a parishioner if she had any family living "around here." She replied, "No, they're in Sioux Center," which is about ten miles away. After talking with more folks, I came to realize that "around here" means "within our township's borders." Back in the Northeast, "around here" meant "in our quarter of the state," or even "in our half." There are many other differences, some of which we are still learning. We have been here four years and are continuing to adjust to this culture. And, yes, we have learned to say, "pop!"

It's normal and natural that my family and I are still learning what it means to be "Iowan." People usually have a hard time comprehending others who are different than they are. It takes work. And sometimes nobody wants to make that effort. How many wars, border disputes, and genocidal campaigns have begun over differences in such things as skin colors, ancestries, religions, and even dialects, often because there was either an unwillingness or an inability to strive for understanding?

> God is different in that he always has the power to accomplish whatever he wants to, while we often live lives of frustration.

What does all this have to do with our dealings with the Lord? Well, God is the One who is ultimately, supremely different than we are. The Bible uses the adjective "holy" to describe God. One definition for "holy" is "different." To say that God is holy is to say that he is different from us. God is different from us in that he has no sin and no weaknesses. God is different from us in that he is immortal and is unbound by time and its constraints. God never gets sick and never grows old. His capabilities never diminish. God is different because we are creatures. He is the uncreated Creator. God is different in that he always has the power to accomplish whatever he wants to, while we often live lives of frustration. God is different because he is the intellect that originated and super-intends the universe, while we have problems programming our VCRs. God is different in that when he makes a promise he is always able to keep it because no future events take him by surprise, while we can plan to go to the soccer game but have to work late instead when the boss tells us to. The Lord is never cranky due to lack of sleep, or depressed because he's on antibiotics. God would never forget where he put his car keys. God doesn't even need a car! It stands to reason, then, that it's going to require some serious effort on our part when we interact with such a Being. He certainly doesn't look at things the same way we do. Some things he does will be as incomprehensible to us as Cricket and Change Ringing are to those outside of Great Britain.

Think of the many questions we Christians ask to which the answer (at least partially) is "God is beyond our understanding," such as:

"How could God allow that accident to happen when he is not the author of evil?"

"Why does the Bible teach election in some passages and free will in others? How can it assert that both are true at the same time?"

"If God is the One who works in us to bring about our sancti-fication, and he empowers us for holiness, then how can we be held responsible when we fall back into sin?"

The answer, "God is beyond our understanding," may seem, at first, to be unsatisfying. We in the Western world want to have everything fully explained to us and to have it all make logical sense. The Eastern peoples have far less trouble with embracing contradiction and mystery than we do. But we are products of our rational, scientific culture. It doesn't seem right to us that there are some things that are beyond our comprehension. And our egos get taken down a peg or two. Our finite, limited creatureliness is suddenly thrown back in our face, and, quite frankly, we don't like it. We want to be like God and understand everything he can. We think it's our right. That was the original temptation, was it not (Genesis 3:1–7)?

So, chances are that you will have to wrestle with God over his answer that goes against your grain. But during the bout, you can be strengthened and taught. I wrestled with the Lord for years over the whole "free will versus predestination" controversy. In the process, I had to ask myself if I really trusted God or only trusted in my limited intellect. Could and would I believe something that didn't make sense to me, in this case that free will and election were somehow compatible in the mind of God, simply because the Word of God said it? Or was I the final arbiter of the truth? Was my motto going to be, "God said it. I believe it. That settles it"? Or, "God said it. I can't fathom it. I'll jettison it"? Eventually, though not without some struggle, I came to accept my creaturehood and my limitations. I had many stimulating discussions with Calvinists, Arminians, and those somewhere in between the theological camps and became close friends with many of them. I can remember having a (mostly) friendly argument with my pastor over some of the verses and points he was using to buttress his own position on the matter when he said to me, "Steve, your fight isn't with me. I didn't say these things. God did. Your fight is with him, and one day you'll decide to surrender and let God be God." He was absolutely right!

Other things about God and Christianity aren't so much incomprehensible as they are alien and nonsensical, at least at first glance. They, too, go against our grain because they seem to be polar opposites to the way our day-to-day world usually operates:

"I can't earn my way into heaven? I have to accept it as a gift? Hey, I work to earn a living, or to make a name for myself, or to win respect! I exercise my body to grow strong! Yet, I can't make it through the pearly gates on my own efforts? That's un-American. Here we lift ourselves up by our own bootstraps. We're 'can do' people!"

> Some things about God go against our grain because they seem to be polar opposites to the way our day-to-day world usually operates.

"I can't look down on the dope addict because there, but for the grace of God, go I? But I'm a better person than he is! I've made good choices!"

"I'm not to take revenge on someone even when it's in my power to do so?"

"One life that's touched through my meager witnessing is equally important to God as the thousands that came forward at a Billy Graham crusade?"

"In order to be happy and fulfilled in life, I must deny myself and take up a cross?"

Throughout our Christian lives we are interacting with the One who is different from us. And that entails some wrestling and some effort in order to understand and accept where the Other is coming from.

Material Girl (or Boy)

Hebrews 11:1 says, "Now faith is being sure of what we hope for and certain of what we do not see." And 2 Corinthians 5:7 reminds us, "We live by faith, not by sight."

In other words, our physical eyes don't give us the whole story. So sometimes we shouldn't trust them. Sometimes what we see will mislead us.

For instance, when everything seems to be going wrong for you, have you ever been tempted to conclude that God doesn't love you, or has abandoned you, or is out to get you? I certainly have! The Bible teaches that none of these things are true, but all our senses yell, "Yes they are! Just look at all the bad things that are happening to me!"

Or what about when a loved one dies? Will he or she live again, or will our friend or family member remain dead, inanimate, forever? What do your sight and your sense of touch tell you at the funeral home? Aren't they giving you a message that contradicts the Word of God? Sometimes when I am conducting the service at the graveyard, a thought flits through my mind that my words about "the sure and certain hope of the resurrection" might seem rather strange in light of the fact that we are gathered around a stone cold dead body inside a sealed coffin that is about to be lowered into an open waiting grave and covered up with a mound of dirt. To make matters worse, surrounding us are tombstones marking the locations of scores of deceased saints who haven't come back to life or gone anywhere for a long, long time. Yet, God calls on us to ignore all that and take him at his Word.

After seminary, when I was still single, I moved into an apartment and began ministering in a city where I knew hardly anyone—particularly anyone my age. Loneliness was a real problem for me during that time of my life. I knew that the Bible asserted that God was always with me, but my eyes couldn't see him and my ears couldn't hear him. My theology tried to tell me that I wasn't sitting all by myself in my apartment on a Friday night, but my senses said, "Look around, Steve! Do you see anybody else here?"

Our senses often come into play, trying to disrupt our concentration or to get us to give up, when we have prayed about something over and over again, and yet haven't seen anything changed. We're tempted to come to erroneous conclusions:

"Prayer doesn't accomplish anything."

"God either doesn't hear me or isn't interested in me."

"God doesn't love me anymore!"

None of these statements are true according to God's Word. But what about what we're observing with our eyes, hearing with our ears, and feeling with our hearts? Well, that's another story altogether.

The Bible calls Christians, who live in the material world of solid objects, space, time, sight, sound, touch, and taste, to believe in ideas, promises, and beings that can't be proven by referencing any of these things. And that's hard work. That entails some wrestling. That means going at it by faith and not by sight!

The Bible gives us even more to wrestle with in this regard. It tells us that the spiritual world, which exists outside of our senses and our experiences, directly affects what takes place in our material world. What happens in that other realm can determine what will come our way today or tomorrow. Yet, unless God reveals to us the activities and decisions of the "higher plane," we have no way of knowing what is going on there. In the book of Job, chapters 1 and 2 make clear that everything Job suffers is a direct result of meetings that God had with some heavenly beings, but Job never finds that out, not even at the end of

> The Bible calls Christians, who live in the material world of solid objects, space, time, and senses to believe in ideas, promises, and beings that can't be proven through any of these things. And that's hard work.

the story! In Daniel 10:1–14, we are given a glimpse of some of the things that take place in that other realm. An answer to the prophet's mournful prayers had been delayed because of spiritual battles taking place that he knew nothing of. And Revelation chapters 4–16 show persecuted Christians that they are not outside of God's care or his plan, but that what they are experiencing is directly related to what heaven and the forces of Satan are doing. If God hadn't revealed this to them, they could have easily jumped to wrong conclusions.

If you've ever served in the military, or worked for a corporation, you probably know what it's like to receive orders from "The Top," but not know how they were arrived at, or what their full ramifications are. The officers or managers had a meeting to map everything out, but you weren't invited. And perhaps you've had to wrestle with those orders somewhat, struggling to obey them even when you really don't understand them. And maybe insights into the minds of your superiors came as you started to see the results of the orders as they were carried out. Or maybe not.

Well, the "Spiritual Boss" and his agents, the angels, are having conferences all the time, and you aren't there. Nobody even told you there *was* a meeting! And they are constantly handing down strategies, memos, orders, and changes to this earthly realm. Sometimes your entire "department" will seem to have been restructured, and you didn't even know anything was coming. You'll have to wrestle with what's happening, and maybe even with your feelings and attitudes toward "The Boss." Perhaps understanding will come as you see how everything plays out. Perhaps not, though.

Most parents, at one time or another, have had to resort to the answer of "Because I said so," when one of their children asked why he or she couldn't do thus-and-so. The child may not be old enough or mature enough to understand the reasons. The child wasn't privy to the long discussion Mommy and Daddy had about the matter, nor could he or she have followed it anyway. Maybe as the child matures, Mommy and Daddy's logic and decision-making processes will start to make sense. Maybe they never will, and someday when the child becomes an adult, he or she will look back through the years and shrug and say, "I could never figure out what was up with Mom and Dad about that."

Often in life, we are compelled to ask questions that boil down to, "What was up with our heavenly Father about that?"

"Why is it that the man on TV was healed, but I wasn't?"

"I can't understand why I didn't get that great new job! I seemed perfect for it and it for me!"

"How come I had to spend most of the mission trip sick in bed?"

"Why did the church I grew up in have to close?"

Maybe, as you wrestle with him over your questions and thereby gain some strength, wisdom, and maturity, the whys and wherefores may start to make sense. But maybe there are some matters you'll never fully understand because you're only a human and God is God. In those cases, after the wrestling, you'll just have to trust him by faith.

> As you wrestle with God over your questions and thereby gain some strength, wisdom, and maturity, the whys and wherefores may start to make sense.

There have been times when members of a congregation I was pastoring have questioned a decision that the church's governing board had made. Though I patiently tried to enable them to see the board's reasoning, a part of me thought, "How can you possibly understand? You didn't hear all that we heard. You don't know all the facts about this issue that we do. Can't you just trust us? Or do you think somehow that when the board meets we all rub our hands together in evil anticipation and cackle, 'How can we destroy the church of Jesus Christ tonight?' while 'The Imperial March' [Darth Vader's theme] from *Star Wars* plays in the background?"

I believe that God has said to me at times, "Can't you just trust me? Do you really imagine that I, who sent Jesus to the cross for you, am assembling my angels and asking, 'How can we really mess up Steve's life this time?'"

I want to trust, and I wrestle in order that I might trust.

It's Your Turn!

Here are some questions to stimulate your own thoughts as you interact with this chapter, either by yourself or in a group.

1. How does the fact that God is different than we are comfort and encourage you? Does it disquiet you in any way?

2. How do you deal with the seemingly unanswerable questions of the Christian life in your day-to-day living?

3. Is there such a thing as "blind faith"? Is it a good thing, or a bad thing?

4. How can you tell the difference between erroneous messages your senses may be sending you and the truth? How can you avoid listening to lies? Sometimes your senses will be telling you the truth. How can you know when this is happening?

5. Has there been a time in your life when your senses and your reason gave you the wrong impression about what was really going on? If you are in a group, can you tell the members about it?

6. Does knowing that there are "meetings" being held in the spiritual realm that affect life on earth calm you or terrify you?

7. Are there any questions or concerns you have after reading this chapter?

Chapter 4

The Ecstasy from the Agony

Even if wrestling with God wasn't inevitable, I'd be more than willing to climb into the ring of my own accord. And I believe that once you discover the benefits of going toe-to-toe with the Almighty, as tough as that may be at times, you'll look forward to hearing those opening bells, too.

Blessed Are the Fighters, for Theirs Is the Kingdom

The Jesus whom many characterize as being "meek and mild," and who promised that God would be with those who are poor in spirit, mourning, and persecuted, also said, "From the days of John the Baptist until now, the kingdom of heaven has been forcefully advancing, and forceful men lay hold of it" (Matthew 11:12). Luke records this same teaching of Jesus in chapter 16, verse 16, "The Law and the Prophets were proclaimed until John. Since that time, the good news of the kingdom of God is being preached, and everyone is forcing his way into it."

Unfortunately, in today's world we are now facing fanatics who firmly believe that their religion demands that they force their ways upon others, even using violence to accomplish their goals, and so we shy away from biblical teachings that can be misconstrued to make it seem that we should do the same. But Jesus isn't calling on us to go on jihads against unbelievers.

What he *is* telling us is that God's kingdom belongs to people who will tackle God and life head-on, vigorously and without flinching. In other words, if you want to enter the kingdom, you're going to have to wrestle with God. Storm the gates of heaven with your prayers! Throw yourself into an in-depth study of the Scriptures, even the troubling, confusing, or hard parts. Immerse yourself in opportunities for ministry and service that will cause you to stretch, question, and grow. Don't let God get away from you. Grab on to him and hold tight!

The vigorous, demanding faith that the Bible presents is quite different from what is sometimes offered in our churches today. While attending a worship service at a church, I found myself unable to enthusiastically join in during the praise singing. The problem was that all of the lyrics of all the songs could be summarized by one of four statements, or some combination of them:

"Jesus makes me feel warm and fuzzy and good inside."

"God gets me all excited."

"Jesus wipes away my tears, applies Band-Aids to my spiritual boo-boos, and helps me forget my problems."

"Heaven will be great when we can sit around loving Jesus and being loved by him forever!"

Ironically, though praise singing had been added to the service in an attempt to reach "the young people," it seemed to me that the content of the songs wasn't really offering the young people anything that would demand their allegiance, or even necessarily get their attention. None of the four statements seemed all that relevant to them, and I could picture "the young people" reacting with yawns.

"Jesus makes me feel warm and fuzzy and good inside." *Big deal. So does necking with my girlfriend or watching a Tom Hanks/Meg Ryan DVD.*

"God gets me all excited." *So does going to a basketball game or waiting in line for that new roller coaster where you ride upside down most of the way.*

"Jesus wipes away my tears, applies Band-Aids to my spiritual boo-boos, and helps me forget my problems." *So do my buddies, a couple of cold cans of beer, and a new, engrossing computer game.*

"Heaven will be great when we can sit around loving Jesus and being loved by him forever!" *Yeah. It'll be just swell. Whoopee. We get to spend eternity with a cosmic Mr. Rogers singing the Barney song, "I love you. You love me. We're a happy family . . ."*

I contrast all this with the teaching I received when I was a "young person." It was during the Jesus Movement of the late sixties and early seventies. Having Jesus as our warm, caring friend, and grooving on God and heaven and all was definitely part of the movement (as it is also admittedly part of the Bible and of the Christian life), but due to great teaching from our church's pastor, Sunday school teachers, and youth leaders, we were also confronted with the Jesus who said, "Let the dead bury the dead," and, "Sell everything you have and follow me," and, "Anyone who loves his father or mother more than me is not worthy of me."

I can remember my pastor facing thirty of us teenagers crowded into his living room and challenging us, "You all say that you're Jesus Freaks now, but I'll bet that in ten years' time there won't be more than five or six of you left still following the Lord. Living for Jesus will just get too tough and unpopular, and you'll drop away." I remember our youth leaders saying, "God wants us to move beyond the singing and the hugging and to start dealing with the sins and wrong ways of thinking that are rooted deep in our hearts, because these things displease him." I can remember talking with other young adults and considering how we could support and encourage one another in the face of persecution and how we could reach our unsaved friends and family members. We were told that we were God's agents of redemption in a world that desperately needed saving, and we tried to live up to our calling, even if it meant that God would have to put us through some painful, unpleasant training at times. We were given a Supreme Being to interact with, even butt heads with. We were given a cause to live for. We were given a faith that demanded our all.

The "young people" from the churches in the geographic area where I attended the praise singing worship service weren't offered that. They were given a bland, wimpy, self-help guru god who demanded nothing more of them than that they try to be happy all the time, and a faith that required nothing—no blood, no sweat, no tears. And they were rejecting that God and that faith in droves, much to the consternation of their parents and congregational leaders.

> We were given a Supreme Being to interact with, even butt heads with. We were given a cause to live for. We were given a faith that demanded our all.

The New Testament essentially says to us, "Here's Jesus. Do you have guts enough to follow him? It's hard going, but it sure beats any alternative." And it assures us that when we find ourselves in hot water because of our faith, or find ourselves wrestling with God about some aspect of our calling, our faith, or our lives, we are part of the kingdom of God. Being willing to step into the ring with the Almighty means that kingdom promises, benefits, and perks are yours, now and into eternity!

What Doesn't Kill Me Makes Me Stronger

When Michael Jordan and Dennis Rodman played for the Chicago Bulls, one of the reasons they were the greatest player in the world and the best rebounder, respectively, was because they would go work out in the weight room *after* the games. When most men would be hitting the showers and looking forward to putting their feet up and relaxing, Jordan and Rodman were exercising. Why? Because they knew that exercising would make them even stronger, even better players. As I write these words, Shaquille O'Neal is the top center in the NBA, not only because of his size, but because he continually works on his game during the off-seasons. As an NBA fan, I have seen him improve year by year because of his dedication and pursuit of excellence.

Jordan, Rodman, and O'Neal realize that in order to stay on top of their game as athletes, they must continually train and exercise. Likewise, if we want to be at our best for the Lord, we will need to continually exercise our spiritual muscles. Paul wrote in 1 Timothy 4:8, "For physical training is of some value, but godliness has value for all things, holding promise for both the present life and the life to come." And I'm not sure how one can become godly without engaging in some wrestling with God!

In my case, as God worked in my heart to make me more like Jesus, he's pressed me to give up hobbies that threatened to take over his rightful place in my life, to search and purify my true motives for what I'm supposedly doing "in his name," and to puzzle over whether some activities were sinful for me to engage in, or harmless. I didn't always obey, or even understand what he was telling me, right away. I had to wrestle. And I know I'll have to wrestle again and again because, as the cliché puts it, "God's not finished with me yet." But that's okay. It means that those parts of me that are harmful to my soul, to God's cause, and to others will continue to be excised from my life, while the parts of me that are what God had in mind when he granted me eternal life will continually get stronger.

Just as athletes grow stronger through physical exercise, so our faith will grow stronger as we exercise spiritually. An athlete will endure the pain and struggle of training, knowing that he or she will be the better off in the long run because of it. Climb into the ring gladly with God. You'll be the better off for it.

Easy Come, Easy Go

Another benefit of getting in the ring with God is that it helps to tie your heart to him. Those who wrestle with God generally find it more difficult to give up on the faith than it is for those who are only nominal Christians, or for those who sort of flirted with God for a while but never seriously engaged him.

While I was attending college and seminary and observing relationships forming and breaking up (not to mention suffering through some of my own romantic affairs of the heart), it seemed to me that those who were trying to carry on "long-distance" romances with someone back home or at another school were more devastated when they received a "Dear John" or a "Dear Sally" letter than the students were who had met someone on campus, dated and gone steady for a while, and then split up. You see, the "long-distance lovers" usually put so much more effort into their relationships than the people who could have lunch and supper together every day in the cafeteria. They had to constantly send letters, cards, and gifts. They had to pay for long-distance phone calls (this was long

> Just as athletes grow stronger through physical exercise, so our faith will grow stronger as we exercise spiritually.

before the days of the Internet, email, and instant messaging).
They planned for trips to see the objects of their affections. They
said No to the "temptations" of other suitable mates living in closer
proximity to them. They invested quite a large chunk of emotional,
spiritual, and even physical change in their relationships, so they
found it very hard to give up those relationships.

After you have wrestled with God and made efforts to get
through to him and to cling to him when the going was rough, you
will find it hard indeed to give up on the faith and to throw your
relationship with him out the window.

As a pastor, I always feel a little suspicious of visitors to my
congregation who proclaim on their first Sunday with us, "This is
the place for me! How do I join?" Usually, these types of people
have a history of church hopping, and the first time they become
disappointed by something in our congregation, they will be out
the door and hitting the road. By contrast, when newcomers who
regularly attend for a while get involved in some aspects of our
ministry, ask questions about our doctrine and practices, take a
new members/inquirers class, and then finally decide to join the
church, they will usually stay with us for the long haul. They've put
forth the effort, and that has cemented the relationship.

When you expend considerable effort wrestling with God, it
will help cement your relationship with him.

Escape from Never-Never Land

Wrestling with God can help you evangelize your friends and
relatives because it authenticates your witness to others.

Once, a well-meaning woman came to see me because she
felt that she was being ineffective for Christ at her place of
employment. I listened to her and soon discovered the problem.
She believed that it was her Christian duty to keep a smile per-

manently plastered on her face and a cheerful song in her heart come what may. But instead of attracting her co-workers to Christ as she had planned, her behavior made them avoid her because they thought something was psychologically wrong with her. She meant for her actions to win people to Christ, but instead her co-workers shook their heads and rolled their eyes, labeling her as someone who didn't live in the "real world." I tried to get her to see that instead of taking, "Rejoice in the Lord always. I will say it again: Rejoice!" as a prooftext to justify her weird behavior, she would have been better off wrestling with just

> How were the thoughts and feelings the apostle Paul was experiencing compatible with rejoicing in the Lord?

what "Rejoice in the Lord always" really meant. I wanted her to think about how the same Paul who wrote that statement could elsewhere express the turmoil he felt over the state of the church and report that he had no peace of mind at Troas because he didn't know what had happened to Titus. How were the thoughts and feelings he was experiencing compatible with rejoicing in the Lord? Wrestling with God over his Word may have also led her to ask why the Lord allowed laments to be recorded in the Bible. She would have been more effective as a witness if she had showed her peers that she faced up to, and was affected by, life's problems, yet still believed in God.

She's not the only Christian who's ever had difficulties facing reality. I knew a man who threw away his glasses, claiming that God had healed his eyesight. Weeks went by and the man, squinting and straining his eyes mightily, kept saying that he knew he was healed and was claiming it. Finally, though, he had to go get new glasses because he was no longer able to see well enough to do his job. God didn't get the glory that the man planned on giving him, but the incident did generate lots of laughs. Maybe the man should have wrestled with the questions of divine healing, why a loving God would permit one of his children to live with an infirmity, and what resources God would provide to help him carry on in a fallen world.

Then there was a long-time member of a congregation who claimed to be receiving messages from God about the state of the church and what it should and shouldn't do. Even though the messages often contradicted themselves and went against the decisions made by the church's leaders, she insisted that she knew the voice of the Lord. Eventually, she was instrumental in ousting the pastor, splitting the congregation apart, and scattering its members hither and yon. No "Praise the Lords" were heard, but there were plenty of sighs and wails over the dissension she had caused. The woman needed to wrestle with how one distinguishes between words of the Lord and personal wants and opinions. She needed a better understanding of the nature of divine revelation, the place of the whole body of Christ in determining authentic messages from God, and that all-important question, "Could I be wrong, Lord?" instead of relying on her feelings and intuitions and voices no one else could hear.

Seekers are looking for a faith that helps them face and deal with, not escape from, reality. They want a religion that is grounded in this world and in the practicalities and challenges of day-to-day living, not one that seems to them to be the phony, "airy fairy" product of a feverish or naive mind that dwells in some sort of personal fantasy realm. They want hope and comfort, yes, but a hope and comfort that transcends, not ignores, pain and disappointment. They will be attracted to someone who can admit, along with Paul, "We are hard pressed on every side, but not crushed; perplexed, but not in despair; persecuted, but not abandoned; struck down, but not destroyed." They are looking for a faith that can "take it" and that can help them "take it" as well.

If you wrestle with God regularly and are willing to talk with others about your wrestling, you will be an effective witness for Jesus Christ.

"This Kind Can Come Out Only by Prayer"

The New Testament tells us about a time when the disciples were stumped. Why was Jesus able to cast an evil spirit out of a boy when they could not? After all, Jesus had previously given them authority over evil spirits! Jesus answered and let them know that their faith was small and that they hadn't been praying enough. Some ancient manuscripts also add that they hadn't been fasting. But no matter what manuscript is used, the main message is the same, namely that the disciples were coasting, so Jesus reminded them that if they wouldn't make any effort, they wouldn't see any miracle. (See Matthew 17:19–21; Mark 6:7, 12–13; 9:28–29.)

I began this book using the biblical story of an Old Testament patriarch putting forth quite an effort dealing with the Lord. In that story about a man physically wrestling with God, Jacob refused to let go of God until God blessed him. The implication is certainly made that if Jacob had given in and given up when God wrenched his hip, Jacob wouldn't have received the blessing. Because Jacob persevered through the pain and the sweating, he obtained what he was looking for.

Blessings such as personal spiritual revivals and even my meeting the woman who would become my wife have come to me after periods of fasting and prayer. God gave me a new job after many days and late nights of crying out to him. Confidence in my position on such controversial subjects as women's ordination, the place of spiritual gifts today, and the end times came to me only after extended periods (in some cases, years!) of serious studying, agonizing, and debating. Once, after setting aside a time for concentrated prayer about a matter, I was denied my request but was given new insight into myself, my God, and his ways.

It's a fact of spiritual life that many spiritual breakthroughs—answered prayer, revival, victory over persistent sin, guidance in a time of crisis, a deeper understanding of biblical truth, a closer relationship with God, a transcendent experience of the Lord's presence—often only come after one has made the effort to wrestle with God and has practiced some, or all, of what will be covered in Part Two of this book. No wrestling, no victory! To receive the blessings God has in store for you, climb into the ring and stay there!

Respect Your Opponent

My only experience with real, classical wrestling as it is done in high schools and colleges (as opposed to professional wrestling and fooling around with my buddies on the lawn) came when I was in twelfth grade. In gym class, we had a very quick unit on wrestling. We spent four or five periods going over the different moves, and then we launched right into the matches. The coach paired us off, and I was scheduled to go against one of

> No wrestling, no victory! To receive the blessings God has in store for you, climb into the ring and stay there!

the school's top athletes, a star of soccer, basketball, and baseball. I wasn't a star athlete. I'm blind in one eye and was born with two left feet. I was a fine arts type of guy, into creative writing and drama. But I did enjoy weight training and our weekend pick-up football games where a big guy like me could at least plow through an offensive line or stand in the way of a runner. Anyway, to make a long story short, I was pretty positive that "The Star" would pin me when we fought, but I was determined that his victory wouldn't be an easy one. And it wasn't. I strained against him and refused to plop my shoulders down onto the mat until, literally, the final seconds of the match. Afterward in the locker room, "The Star" looked at me wonderingly and said, "Man, Steve, (we all said, "Man," back then) you are really strong!" Throughout the rest of the day, I would see him with his jock buddies out of the corner of my eye. He would be pointing at me, and I'd overhear him expressing amazement that I was stronger than he expected me to be. His comments made me feel so good that it almost made up for the fact that my limbs continued to shake, I was totally nauseous, and I suddenly believed that it would be a good plan to get on my hands and knees and slowly crawl my way to the rest of the day's classes!

I gained a new respect from "The Star" that day. And I find that this is the same kind of thing that wrestling with God does for me—it gives me a new respect for the Almighty.

In grappling with God over the hard questions and circumstances of life in general, and my life in particular, I realize just how strong the Lord is and how weak I am by comparison. I come face-to-face with the fact that although I'm seminary trained and have had forty-seven years on this earth, there is still much about God, the Bible, myself, life, the universe, and everything that I don't, and cannot, know. God is infinitely inexhaustible! And there is much about my life and my future, despite whatever plans I make, that is totally beyond my control. It's in the hands of One much more powerful than I am.

These realizations are good, for they force me to humbly acknowledge my utter dependence upon God and to keep turning to him for the help, strength, and guidance that he is more than willing to give. Life really is too much for me. But it's not too much for him.

In This Corner, the Masked Marvel!

One of the staples of professional wrestling is fighters who appear in disguises. Who are they really? Everyone wants to know, and speculation runs rampant. Then the inevitable day finally comes when they either willingly unmask in public, or are defeated and exposed at the hands of their opponent.

We'll experience times when we think we're wrestling with God, but we're really struggling with Satan and his demonic forces, or our own sinful tendencies, or the world, in disguise. The wrestling match, by focusing us on our problems and questions and bringing them before the Lord, gives us the opportunity to unmask our foes. Then, having

> When a match with God is over, you will definitely be changed.

seen them for who and what they truly are, we can make the preparations we'll need in order to defeat them.

"Why is God doing this to me?!" Maybe the only part God had to play was setting up the rule that actions have consequences. Maybe you are where you're at today because of all the choices you've made along the way. Or maybe you're experiencing what it's like to live in a fallen, imperfect world, handed down to us from our father, Adam. Or maybe you are under demonic attack.

"Why did God take that young girl away?" God didn't. The drunk driver, or the cancer, or the fire did.

"What is God trying to teach me through this?" Maybe nothing. Maybe it's really Satan trying to tempt and break you.

"Who is God trying to punish in all this?" Maybe no one. Sigmund Freud once became weary of people trying to find hidden psychological meaning and symbolism in everything and stated that sometimes a cigar is just a cigar. We need to be careful about seeing God's discipline in places where it doesn't exist. One of the reasons that the Bible gives for bad things occurring is, "Sometimes things just happen. There's no deep spiritual significance to them." (See Luke 13:1–5 and 1 Timothy 5:23. In the latter verse, notice that Paul doesn't blame Timothy's medical problems on sin, or worry, or lack of trust in God, or not enough prayer. He just matter-of-factly mentions it and prescribes a matter-of-fact medicinal aid that may help.)

There are many advantages to engaging in spiritual wrestling, and when a match with God is over, you will definitely be changed. But how do you know when it's over? We'll explore this question next.

It's Your Turn!

Here are some questions to stimulate your own thoughts as you interact with this chapter, either by yourself or in a group.

1. How do you react to the image of the Christian being forceful and forcing his or her way into the kingdom? Does this negate the concept of grace?

2. Has your involvement with the ministry and mission of God's people strengthened your faith in God? How? And if it hasn't, why not?

3. What are the most important characteristics and qualities an "attractive witness" for Jesus Christ should have? What were some of the people who led you to Christ, or helped you grow in the faith, like?

4. Has there ever been a time when the forces opposing you have been unmasked either by yourself, or by others, or by God? If you are in a group, can you tell the others about it?

5. Are there other benefits of wrestling with God that weren't mentioned in this chapter? Which of the benefits in this chapter have you personally experienced?

6. How can wrestling with God be seen as evidence of faith in God?

7. Are there any questions or concerns you have after reading this chapter?

Chapter 5

The Buzzer Sounds

A wrestling match with God can end in one of four possible ways, or some combination of them. Let's take a look at each of the four, beginning with the outcome we usually hope for when we enter the ring.

Possible Outcome — You Win!

You're singing the old Gospel standard "V Is for Victory" because your prayers have been answered, or a stubborn sin was conquered, or your hard questions have been dealt with, or your resolve has been strengthened, or you have experienced a renewed sense of the presence of God, or your circumstances have been changed, or whatever! Something happened so that you, like Jacob, received your "blessing."

I think back on two times in my life when I added another mark to my "win" column. I was twenty-eight years old and still single. I had watched friend after friend get married. Always a best man, never a bridegroom, that was me. And I didn't much like it. As the years slipped by, some well-meaning people, most of them already married, engaged, or involved, counseled me to find contentment as a single person. Finding their advice very ironic, I, nonetheless, prayed that God would give me peace about being single. Yet, at the same time, I couldn't fully believe that I would ever have peace, because, as I studied the Bible and what it had to say about singleness and marriage, I became convinced that I was not the kind of person God was calling to be a solo act. True, there are those who, for the sake of the kingdom, decide to be celibate (Matthew 19:11–12; 1 Corinthians 7:3–9, 36–38) and find they have lots of time to give to God's concerns. But as for me, far from being able to focus more on spiritual things than married folk could, I was constantly tempted by Satan, my hormones, my mind, and the world. I also couldn't escape the fact that God had said way back in the book of Genesis that it wasn't good for man to be alone, and in my profession, the pastorate, I was often lonely because I was far from family and friends, ministering to people who were essentially strangers. How I shouted, "Amen!" to Genesis 2:18.

So there I was, wrestling with God—wanting to honor him and to submit to his will by being at peace with where he had brought me in life, while his Word seemed to be telling me that I'd never be happy or escape frustration until I was married! But if God wanted me married, why didn't I ever find a relationship that grew into a solid commitment? Couldn't he, the all-powerful One, do *something* to either change me or change my situation? I found myself praying for contentment *and* for change *at the same time!* And, finally, at long, long last, God acted. I met the woman who is now my wife at a time when we were both ready for marriage. I was ecstatic that God had granted the desires of my heart, and at the same time, I could, reluctantly perhaps at first, see that he was wise in having me wait.

The second instance occurred early in my ministry, when the elders of my congregation and I began to suspect that a member of the church might be demon-possessed. This is not a suspicion that leaders in the Presbyterian/Reformed tradition come to lightly, nor do we mention to counselees that we think they are controlled by evil spirits unless we're real sure of what we're talking about. And being good Presbyterian/Reformed churchmen, we weren't real sure, since we never really had to deal with anything like that before. For several days, I threw myself into a thorough study of the subject. I read all the books I had in my library dealing with demons and possessions. The scope of those volumes ranged from claims that that sort of thing went out with the apostolic age to accounts of demons being cast out of articles of clothing and lurking behind almost every corner. I looked up all the Bible verses that mentioned Satan, demons, and possession and consulted my commentaries. I furiously scribbled notes, praying that God would make our next action clear to us. It was an intoxicating experience to immerse myself in the Bible so intensely. It was also a terrifying experience when a large black spider suddenly landed on my shoulder as I was reading an account of an exorcism. I leaped in the air and let out a howl that didn't sound at all like, "Praise the Lord!" But in the end, God did indeed grant us clarity and spiritual discernment, and we came to see that the young man didn't fit the biblical definition of demon possession. He was listening to the wrong voices and giving in to the temptations they presented, to be sure, but he wasn't controlled by them. Through the effort we made by wrestling (not to mention one squashed spider), God had answered our prayers.

Possible Outcome — You Lose!

It's often hard to have God say No to you, particularly if you have put a lot of effort into wrestling with him over a question, concern, or situation. Ask families and churches that have prayed fervently for a critically ill loved one to recover, only to end up filing past a casket in the funeral home. But, often, those people will tell you that although God didn't grant their request and they didn't obtain the end that they desired, still they came to experience God's strength and his mercy in new ways. This is how it was with the apostle Paul when he prayed for a healing, in his case his own. Though his illness wasn't terminal, it was chronic, and he says that it tormented him. He even calls it a "messenger of Satan," and those of us with recurring or unceasing health problems certainly know why! "Messenger of Satan" even seems like too mild a term at times! Paul wrestled with God to have his "thorn in the flesh" removed, pleading

> It's often hard to have God say No to you, particularly if you have put a lot of effort into wrestling with him over a question, concern, or situation.

with the Lord three times. But God didn't remove it. Instead, he told Paul, "My grace is sufficient for you, for my power is made perfect in weakness," and led the apostle to boast about his weaknesses, through which the power of Christ could shine. He helped Paul to view the thorn as an instrument to keep him humble (2 Corinthians 12:7–10).

In my case, though I often wish God had said Yes to removing my own "thorns," I have, sometimes grudgingly and reluctantly to be sure, admitted that they force me to keep relying on God for the energy and strength to do my job as a pastor. God has also said No to me about many relationships, possible job offers, dreams, and priorities. And I wish I could say that I've always instantly accepted defeat gracefully. Sometimes, it's only later on, when I've gained some distance and perspective (often by wrestling with God again), that I can see lessons learned from a No or benefits applied to my life. Perhaps it's like a team that loses the Superbowl or another "big game." Right after it happens, they are devastated and aren't in the mood to view the game films. Later, though, the coach can show them what they did wrong and how to improve.

He even can use the defeat to motivate the team to come back and try harder the next season.

There will be times when God will refuse to grant your wishes. His No answers come in as many varieties as our requests for blessings do. He may overcome all the objections you have to seeing things his way. He may find a way to overpower you and bring you face-to-face with a sin you were unaware of in order that you may repent (2 Samuel 12; Acts 26:12–18). He may force you to resign yourself to the fact that the only thing that's going to change in your present situation is you. He may give you the same answer he gave Paul and help you to be content with it. But for sure he will grant you the same grace he gave to Paul. Whatever he does and however it happens, you will be left with a definite impression that God has "pinned you" and has emerged the victor. And often you will be changed for the better because of it.

Possible Outcome — It's a Tie!

In some matches with God, there are no clear-cut winners. In this kind of a match, there will be days and moments when you seem to be on top, others when it looks like God's got you in a headlock. So you and God will have to keep at it, perhaps indefinitely. Maybe instead of calling such a match a "tie," it would be better to think of it as an ongoing bout.

The Bible is the story of the people of God's ongoing bout with the Lord. In the Old Testament, they took their name from their father, Israel (we knew him first as Jacob), which means, "He struggles with God." And that's certainly what the Jewish people did throughout the entire Old Testament, into the New, and will continue to do until Romans 11 is fulfilled. Lest we Gentile believers get too cocky, though, let's remember that the New Testament teaches that we are the New Israel, in other words, "The new people who struggle with God." Maybe we'll keep struggling for all eternity. Even the souls of the martyrs in heaven awaiting the Second Coming cry out to God with a question, "How long, Sovereign Lord, holy and true, until you judge the inhabitants of the earth and avenge our blood?" (Revelation 6:9–10)!

Many who have experienced tragedy in their lives know what it's like to have an ongoing bout with God. At some moments, they may realize that there are other ways to look at what has befallen them rather than to place the blame on God. At other moments, though, they may say, "But God could have done something to intervene, and yet he chose not to!" Sometimes they will accept that God must have had some valid reasons not to have intervened, and that some good has come from the tragedy, and that they have to trust God when their understanding fails them. But then,

> Many who have experienced tragedy in their lives know what it's like to have an ongoing bout with God.

they find themselves thinking the unthinkable: God is either untrustworthy or wasn't in control of what was going on. Some moments it will be, "I know God loves me because he proved it in the cross of Jesus Christ, and he's sustaining me even now." At others, "Why did God spare those people and not me or my loved one? Does he love them more than me?" They can go from "I'm stronger now and I'm dealing with everything just fine," to "I don't think I can take this pain anymore!" in the blink of an eye. I know from personal experience that such people may have to wrestle with God over their tragedies all of their lives and never reach the place where they can say, "It's all over now."

I have wrestled with God for years over the way my exit from one of my churches came about. Let me make a long story short. At a pastors' conference I once heard a speaker sheepishly admit,

"Church discipline is biblical and necessary, but there's only one problem with it. It doesn't work!" That was the case in my congregation. The leadership and I reluctantly, after a very long period of time trying to forgive, forget, and persevere, took the first steps to discipline a member. (Though I don't mind wrestling with God, I'm not all that keen on confrontations and arguments with humans!) But that had never been done before in that church! Long-standing members were scandalized and began to view what had happened as a "plot" by the newcomers to take over and remove the old guard from power. Nothing could have been further from the truth. Lots of fruitless meetings and sleepless nights ensued. In the end, I left to save my sanity. While I can now see lessons I've learned from everything that happened, I still have to admit that, a lot of the time, I think I'd probably handle things the same way if I had to do it all over again. And I can know that the Lord moved me and others in the congregation away to places where we could minister, but I still have my moments when I wonder why we all couldn't have continued to minister effectively in that location. On "good days" I can see God's hand in everything that happened. On "bad days" I think God was sitting on his hands when it all fell apart. Often I can see logical reasons for God allowing the events to transpire as they did, but, just as often, it seems to me as though chaos ruled. I can go for long periods of time without thinking once of that church and then suddenly find myself spending an entire day brooding about it. Obviously, though my exit took place quite a while ago, it's not yet "over" in my heart, and I'm still engaged in an ongoing bout with God over it.

Others may have ongoing bouts with God over persistent sins, or over a relationship with him that seems to be in a constant holding pattern, or over theological or personal "Why?" questions that remain unanswered, or over doubts that keep coming back, or over prayer that seems to be in accordance with his will, yet yields no results, or over persons and people groups who seem to be resistant to the Gospel, or over a church that seems to continually prefer tradition over the Holy Spirit's leading, or over desires that seem totally legitimate but that seemingly won't be fulfilled this side of the pearly gates, or over different points of contention.

In a tie, nothing seems to really change, not even you, and so it becomes necessary to keep climbing back into the ring again and again.

Possible Outcome — You're Injured!

Though Jacob received his blessing, he limped away from his wrestling match with God because of a wrenched hip socket (Genesis 32:25, 31–32). Though Job finally gained the audience with God he desperately sought and had his prestige and prosperity restored (Job 42), still he had lost seven sons and three daughters (Job 1).

> Some carry scar tissues and injuries from wrestling with God. There are various ways one can become injured when contending with him.

Some carry within their hearts and souls scar tissues and injuries from wrestling with God. There are various ways one can become injured when contending with the Lord. Here are a few examples of wounded warriors:

- A young Christian, full of enthusiasm, joined a church. Here was a place of love, acceptance, and refuge. The people of God. Here all could joyfully use their gifts in service for Jesus and work alongside of others who were doing the same. But after she had been a member for a while, she overheard some people complaining about the workload, others criticizing the leaders, still others gossiping about members not present, and others squabbling about the "right" way to put on a church dinner. Her tender heart was broken, and her soul was in turmoil. "It's not supposed to be like this, God! Should I keep coming back here? Have I believed a lie? How can people sing, 'They'll Know We Are Christians by Our Love' one minute and stick knives into their neighbors' backs the next?" The new Christian struggled through to the answers and discovered that God was calling her to love sinners just as he does, that the Bible never teaches that the church is perfect, and that perseverance is a fruit of the Spirit. But there was still definitely a sense of the loss of innocence. Hopefully, that pain in her heart will continue to transform itself into a deep longing for Christ's return when all will be perfected and the church purified. And, hopefully, it can spur her onward to work at making her congregation all that it can be.

- Some have found that their wrestling with God has led them to the opposite conclusion than the young Christian came to. They have been called to leave congregations because of doctrinal issues, or increased opportunities for ministry elsewhere, or to escape bitter, unproductive "church fights," or for other legitimate reasons. While they knew that they were doing the right thing, they still experienced the pain of separating from the familiar and from friends and/or family members.

- Others have found that, in the course of their bouts, God revealed to them that they weren't as smart or as mature or as holy as they thought they were. When our cherished self-delusions are ripped away, it hurts! Who really enjoys facing up to the fact that they are sinners, make mistakes, and could very well be responsible for the jams they find themselves in?

- Obedience to the Lord and finally determining his will after sparring with him have led some to break up relationships when they realized that bad company was corrupting good character, or that their goals and desires were very different from other people's, or that there was no future down the road they were heading, or that the relationships in the long run would be destructive to all parties involved. Some have found that, as they wrestled with God over relationships, the other parties initiated the breakups on their own! (I know. It's happened to me. "Er . . . this isn't quite what I had in mind, Lord!") But, in any case, they experienced the pains of loneliness, uncertainty, betrayal, and/or a lost love.

Pain can be redemptive, though. When the old injuries flare up, they can help you to be sensitive and empathetic to those who are going through similar suffering now, so that you'll be able to comfort them with the same comfort you received after your injury (2 Corinthians 1:3–7). Just as a retired wrestler may remember a certain match whenever his trick knee bothers him, you may find yourself remembering encounters with God when your soul experiences a twinge. And as a wrestler might say something like, "I should have used my legs more when lifting my opponent," while gingerly rubbing his back, so one who has grappled with the Almighty might remember the lessons he or she learned in the process, as he or she now massages his or her aching heart with psalms, hymns, and spiritual songs.

A wise, older pastor told me, as I studied for the ministry, that in order to be a good pastor, one has to have gone through some suffering. Otherwise, pastors can remain aloof and detached from real life, unsympathetic and unapproachably judgmental toward the people God has called them to shepherd. I have heard many "horror stories" from people who tried to explain their problems, their pains, and their emotions to pastors who summarily dismissed them with, "Well, you're obviously not trusting God," or, "You must have a secret sin in your life," or, "Jesus said that in this world we would have many troubles," or, "Just rebuke Satan and move on." Pain and suffering soften up a pastor's heart and make him or her sensitive to what others are going through and allow for a real meeting of the hearts, minds, and souls to take place so that real help can be offered. Pain and suffering can be beneficial to all Christians in this regard, whether they are ordained or not.

However, pain can drive one away from the Lord, if he or she doesn't understand that the nature of our relationship with God is one of wrestling. For such a person, pain or suffering is unexpected and shocking. He or she believes in a loving God, after all. Rather than realizing that bumps, bruises, pulled muscles, and scrapes are often signs that a loving God is interacting with them, healing them, and spurring them on to grow, some people believe injuries indicate that the Lord has abandoned them. These people let pain cripple them, instead of just hobbling them. The kind of people I'm speaking of are those who no longer affiliate with any congregation because of bad experiences they've had with "hypocrites," or who point to unanswered prayers as proof that there isn't any God, or who had their faith shaken when a college philosophy professor asked tough questions they didn't have an answer for. Pain has left them vulnerable. It's the church's job to love them back to spiritual health and to gently instruct them that aches and pains are part of a healthy spiritual life. As the weight lifters say, "No pain, no gain!"

We'll examine the pains, gains, victories, and defeats of those in the Bible who wrestled with God in our next two chapters and let those wrestling All-Stars teach us how it's done.

It's Your Turn!

Here are some questions to stimulate your own thoughts as you interact with this chapter, either by yourself or in a group.

1. How does one accept it when God says No without constantly wishing for a different outcome or dreaming up "what if" scenarios?

2. How can you tell the difference between losing and a tie? When should you continue to persevere in prayer, and when should you stop?

3. Why wouldn't winning all the time be good for us?

4. How has pain been redemptive in your life?

5. Do you know people who have let pain drive them away from God? How might you minister to them?

6. Which of the possible outcomes of wrestling matches with God have you personally experienced? If you are in a group, can you tell the others about them?

7. Are there any questions or concerns you have after reading this chapter?

Part Two:

How to Do It

Chapter 6

The Old Testament All-Star Team

Let me introduce you to wrestlers from the Old Testament whom I've inducted into "The Spiritual Wrestling Hall of Fame." I'll tell you their stories because there's nothing like watching the masters do it in order to learn how. I hope you'll see that the characters in the Bible weren't all that different from you and me. When we struggle with God, we're not experiencing anything unusual. We're participating in something very common to believers down through the centuries.

So, without further ado, with Bibles in hand, let's meet the All-Stars!

"Awesome" Abraham (a.k.a. Abram)

Abram was the spiritual father of us all, so it is appropriate that he's the first spiritual wrestler we'll examine. Abram was given a tremendous promise by the Lord himself in Genesis 15. God told him that he would become the father of more descendants than anyone could possibly count and that he and they would inherit the land where he now roamed as a nomad and an alien. In verse 6 we read about Abram's response to this promise, reported in the words that form the foundation of our salvation: "Abram believed the LORD, and he credited it to him as righteousness." Er . . . that is, he believed the Lord, sort of. Just two verses down, Abram asks God how he can know for sure that the promise will come true. (Notice his response, as is often the case with the characters in the Bible, is not, "God said it, I believe it, that settles it," but rather, "God said it, I have troubles with it, I'll ask him about it.")

The Lord gives Abram a strange answer. He says, "Bring me a heifer, a goat and a ram, each three years old, along with a dove and a young pigeon" (verse 9). Huh? What's up with that? Is God planning on starting a zoo? Or is he hungry? No, the Lord wants Abram to cut them in two and to arrange the pieces so that the halves are facing opposite of each other. Then Abram had to drive away the birds of prey that came down to feast on the blood and the raw meat. "As the sun was setting, Abram fell into a deep sleep, and a thick and dreadful darkness came over him" (verse 12). Then the Lord outlined the future of Abram's descendants. They would be oppressed slaves in a foreign country (hence the dreadful darkness Abram experienced), but God promised to liberate them, make them prosperous, and return them to the Promised Land as his holy, conquering army to punish the idolatrous nations living there. In light of this information, Abram could be assured that he really would have descendants, because God had their future all mapped out.

But the Lord wasn't finished yet. He gives Abram even more assurance. The Lord goes through a ceremony in front of Abram that meant that he was making a covenant, a solemn promise, with Abram. Verse 17 tells us that "a smoking firepot with a blazing torch appeared and passed between the pieces." That firepot represented the Lord. God was symbolically saying, "If I break my promise to you, Abram, may I be torn into pieces as these animals have been."

Wow! That beats "cross my heart" any day, doesn't it? Abram had received his answer from the Lord—and a dramatic one it was, too! But Abram first had the wisdom, maybe even the audacity, to ask God for it. Yet he had to exert some effort in order to obtain it. We may not have to take a sword to animals in order to have our faith bolstered, but we do need to ask God for assurance, and then we have to do our part to receive it—studying the Bible, learning from other Christians, and stepping out and trying new things in faith.

After Abram and his wife tried to fulfill the promise their own way by having Abram and his slave girl, Hagar, conceive a baby (Genesis 16), God spoke to him again (Genesis 17). Abram was now ninety-nine, and his wife, Sarai (a.k.a. Sarah), was ninety. Nonetheless, God said that the

> We need to ask God for assurance, and then we have to do our part to receive it.

two of them would have a son together and that he would be the child through whom the promise would begin to come to fruition. (This was symbolized in God's changing Abram's name to Abraham.) And Abram/Abraham's response? Genesis 17:17 tells us that he "fell facedown; he laughed and said to himself, 'Will a son be born to a man a hundred years old? Will Sarah bear a child at the age of ninety?'"

The great spiritual wrestling All-Stars of the past were very honest with their reactions and feelings in front of God. They didn't try to cover up, put on acts, use proper courtly manners, or speak with "thee's" and "thou's" lest a "Great and Powerful Oz" lop their heads off. But sometimes we, in our zeal to pay God the proper respect and acknowledge his superiority and place as King of the universe, go too far and put on masks before him, making it hard for him to have a real relationship with us and for us to have one with him. After Abraham composes himself, he expresses his wish to God that the good Lord would forget all this nonsensical talk about Sarah and him having a child and bless instead his son, Ishmael, whom he had with Hagar, his wife's slave woman. But Abraham loses this bout with the Lord when God reiterates that it is Sarah who will bear him the son of promise, not Hagar. However, Abraham also wins, in a sense, because God says that he has heard Abraham, and that Ishmael, the slave woman's son, would also be blessed and that the Lord would make him into a great nation (verse 20).

Another time, in Genesis 18, the Lord and two angels come to have a meal with Abraham. Could there be any more proof needed that God wants to have a relationship with humans? After all, if God showed up at your door around supper time and sat down at your table, wouldn't you think he wanted to have a relationship with you? But the biblical account offers us a further proof, because after they eat, they all walk toward Sodom and the Lord says, "Shall I hide from Abraham what I am about to do?" (verse 17). He says that Abraham will become great because the Lord has chosen him and that Abraham will direct his children to do what is right and just. So God tells Abraham his plan. He's going to judge the twin cities of Sodom and Gomorrah for their wickedness.

Now, Abraham has a relative living in Sodom, but rather than writing him off, saying, "Well, I guess that's the end of poor Lot," Abraham begins to bargain with God. He asks God if he would spare Sodom as long as fifty righteous people could be found in it. God says that he would spare the whole city for the sake of fifty. Abraham proceeds then to bargain the Lord down to ten righteous people. God, in his wisdom, allowed Abraham to have a part in forming the Lord's plan. What an awesome thought! If God—who is the same yesterday, today, and tomorrow, and knows the future, yet somehow, as incomprehensible as it may seem to us—allowed Abraham to do this, doesn't it make sense to believe that he will allow us to have a part in forming his plans, through prayer and wrestling, for ourselves and our loved ones? It lends an urgency and immediacy to spiritual wrestling, does it not? And, would-be wrestling All-Stars should pay special attention to the way Abraham bargains God down. He bases his pleas on the Lord's character. Would it be right for God to kill the righteous along with the wicked? Does that sound like something that the "Judge of all the earth" should do (verses 23–25)? As Abraham bargains, he prefaces his remarks by humbly acknowledging that he is "nothing but dust and ashes" and he requests that, though he has been bold to speak to the Lord, the Lord not be angry with him (verses 27–32).

Spiritual All-Stars know that they contend with the Almighty only by divine sufferance and by his mercy. It's like when I was wrestling with my toddlers. If I wanted to, I could have overpowered my children easily. But because I wanted the game to continue, and wanted to interact with my children and build relationships, I would hold back. Abraham is saying here, "Thanks for holding back, Lord. Now let me try this move on you."

Gorgeous Jake

Jacob was a quiet, fair-skinned, stay-at-home mama's boy who, nonetheless, had a fighting spirit. He had even fought with his twin brother while the two of them were still in their mother's womb! As the boys grew, Jacob couldn't compete with his brother, Esau, physically, but in the areas of craftiness and guile, he outstripped him. First, he swindled his brother out of his birthright. Then Jacob disguised himself and lied to his father in order to get the blessing that rightfully belonged to his brother. As you might imagine, losing his blessing because of Jacob's deceit didn't sit too well with Esau, so Jacob went on the lam. Years later, God told Jacob to go back home. Jacob did so, not knowing how his brother, Esau, would receive him, especially after he heard that Esau was coming to meet him with four hundred men! Still, Jacob knew that God was in the region because angels met him (Genesis 32:1–2). He prayed that the Lord would protect him, reminding God that he was the One who had told Jake to return in the first place and that God had promised that Jake would prosper and that his descendants would be numerous (verses 9–12). But Jake also took what action he could to pacify Esau, sending gifts on ahead so that Esau would receive them before encountering Jacob (verses 13–21).

As great spiritual wrestlers are waiting for God to answer prayer, they know they can attempt to use their own resources to change their situation, or to figure out what the answer to a question may be. Later, after the match, as they review and meditate on all that has taken place, and consider what the Bible teaches about the Lord, they may see that he was at work answering their prayers through their own efforts. They come to understand that what they thought at first were only their own actions were really also the Lord doing his thing at the same time.

> Great spiritual wrestlers come to understand that what they thought at first were only their own actions were really also the Lord doing his thing at the same time.

That night Jacob wanted to be alone. Sometimes, one needs to clear the deck of all distractions and just get down and dirty with God. Jake "got down" with God, all right, because Genesis 32:24 tells us that "a man" wrestled with him until daybreak. The man couldn't overpower Jake, even after touching the socket of his hip and wrenching it. Jacob hung in there and said, "I will not let you go unless you bless me" (verse 26). All-Stars know that, at times, their opponent, God, will seem as if he's trying to get away from them. They cling to him for all they're worth and let nothing shake them loose. The man then gave Jake a new name, Israel, because he had struggled with God and had overcome. However, lest Jacob get a swelled head and go around saying, "Who da man? I da man! I whipped God good!" the stranger let Jake know who was really in charge all the time by refusing to tell Jake his name. And Jacob got the message and was grateful that the Lord held back. He marveled that "I saw God face to face, and yet my life was spared" (verse 30). And that day he was reconciled to Esau.

Joseph "Kid Braggart" Israelson

While Scripture doesn't record for us any actual incidents of Joe wrestling with God, it doesn't take much reading between the lines to believe that he must have done so a time or two. He started out as a brash, spoiled young man who told the rest of his family of his dreams that one day they would all bow down to him. Soon, to the surprise of Joseph, but not to anyone who knows human nature, his jealous brothers had enough of his bragging and stripped him of his fancy clothes and dumped him into an empty well. Later, they sold him into slavery to a caravan heading for Egypt. At this point, Joseph had to be wondering what was going on and whatever had happened to his cool supernatural dreams. However, even through the bad times, he seemed to have a close relationship with the Lord, and he probably sought God regarding his future many times. Then God caused him to prosper as a slave in Potiphar's house in Egypt. Things were beginning to look up!

But things got worse again for Joe. His master's wife kept coming on to him, and when he refused her lewd advances on the grounds that to give in and do such a wicked thing would be to sin against God (Genesis 39:9), she framed him for rape. (Hell hath no fury like a woman scorned!) So Joseph was thrown into prison. But he had held on to God and the Lord's ways even when it may have been more immediately convenient to do otherwise.

On the surface, though, it looked to Joseph as if God, his faith, and his integrity hadn't done him much good. He had landed in prison for doing right. Again, he probably wondered in prayer what was happening. Then the Lord helped him find favor and success even during his stint in jail. When two of Pharaoh's ex-officials, who had also been incarcerated, experienced disturbing dreams, Joe interpreted them. The chief cupbearer's dream meant that he would soon be released and restored to his former position. Joseph asked the cupbearer to put in a good word for him with Pharaoh when it happened so that Joe could finally get his freedom. The cupbearer, however, had a lapse in memory and didn't mention Joe to Pharaoh.

Joe had to stay in the prison for two more years, no doubt trying to determine just what God was up to during that time. But then Pharaoh had some very troubling dreams of his own that nobody could explain. The cupbearer finally remembered good old Joe and had him brought before Pharaoh. Joseph told Pharaoh that the dream was a warning from God of a coming famine that would last seven years. Joe also came up with a good plan to save the people of Egypt from starvation and to strengthen the Pharaoh's already considerable power. Becoming an important and respected man in the land as a result, Joseph did indeed see his brothers bow down before him when, at their father's bidding, they traveled from Canaan to Egypt in order to obtain famine relief. After testing them to see if they had learned their lesson and were repentant for what they had done to him twenty years before, Joseph reconciled with them, kissing them and weeping over them, assuring them that God had worked through even all the bad that had happened to save his people from hunger (Genesis 45; 50:19–21).

Joe had looked back over his up-and-down life and come to the conclusion that it was all for the best. Anyone who could have done that had to have spent some time wrestling with God! And doesn't a lot of our spiritual wrestling center on our trying to make sense of what has happened in our lives? Why did God allow such-and-such to happen? I know *my* wrestling does!

Moses "The Liberator"

Big Moe, whom many believe bore a resemblance to a young Charlton Heston, delivered his people from slavery in the land of Egypt. But when God first gave him the job of liberator, he didn't want it. In Exodus, chapters 3 and 4, Moses wrestles with God over his calling by raising objections and asking "what if" questions.

> Doesn't a lot of our spiritual wrestling center on our trying to make sense of what has happened in our lives?

God answers Moses every single time until Moe doesn't have anything left to say except, "You know best, Lord. I humbly submit." Just kidding! Actually, Moses says, "O Lord, please send someone else to do it" (4:13). But God wants Moses, and Moses he shall have. Score one for the Lord!

But evidently after their initial bout, Moe still had trouble submitting to the divine will. In Exodus 4:24–26, we find a very strange story. As Moses was on the way back to Egypt to carry out his mission and free God's people, "the LORD met Moses and was about to kill him." Did you catch that? The Lord was going to kill Moses! Why? Because Moe and his wife hadn't circumcised their son. In other words, the one who was to liberate and lead the Hebrews hadn't obeyed God's commandment to the Hebrews. Moses didn't seem ready yet to adopt Hebrew ways and be totally submissive to the Hebrews' God. But after this hair-raising escape from death, we have every indication that Moses learned his lesson well. Wouldn't you? God pinned Moses down tight. Score another round for the Lord!

Later on, though, Moses won a round, too. While he was with the Lord up on Mount Sinai receiving the Ten Commandments, the Israelites made an idol out of gold in the shape of a calf and worshiped it and had a high old time. The Lord was fed up with the people's wayward bent toward idolatry. In Exodus 32:10, the Lord said to Moses, "Now leave me alone so that my anger may burn against them and that I may destroy them. Then I will make you into a great nation." Notice that the Lord tells Moses to leave him alone. In other words, "My mind is made up. I'm carrying out my plan now. Don't bug me or argue with me or try to talk me out of it." But Moses does just that! In verses 11–13, he tells God that the destruction of his chosen people will make the Lord look bad in the eyes of the Egyptians, and he reminds him of his promise to Abraham, Isaac, and Israel. Verse 14 tells us, "Then the LORD relented and did not bring on his people the disaster he had threatened." The skillful spiritual wrestlers know that sometimes when the Lord seems to be saying, "Let me go," they've got to hang on even more tightly, and that sometimes when he says, "Stop bugging me," it's actually the time to pray harder.

In Numbers 14, there is another account of Moses talking God out of destroying the people and starting over with just Moses. Once again, Moses let the Lord know how bad this would look to the other nations and requested forgiveness for the Israelites based on the character of the Lord—"slow to anger, abounding in love and forgiving sin and rebellion" (verse 18). And then in chapter 16, Moses and his brother, Aaron, again stop the Lord from wiping out everyone, by arguing that an entire nation shouldn't perish for the sins of one man and by making atonement for the people.

Throughout Big Moe's tenure as the leader of the Israelites, he would bring his questions, requests for blessings, complaints, doubts, and frustrations right to God, haggling, bargaining, and wrestling all the way (Exodus 33:1–34:9; Numbers 11:1–25; 12; 20:1–13; 21:1–9; 27). Wrestling with the divine was his way of life.

Gideon "You Must Be Joking" Joashson

When God first contacted Gideon and told him that the Lord was with him, Gideon's response was essentially, "How can that be when we've fallen into the hands of Midian?" In Gideon's mind, if God's people were oppressed by a foreign power, God couldn't possibly be with them. The Lord must have been glad that Gideon asked that question because he tells Gideon that he's sending him to save Israel from Midian. Gid's response was the same as Moses'—he raises an objection that the Lord answers. Then Gideon asks God for a sign so that he knows that it's really the Lord who is speaking to him. God doesn't seem to mind Gid's request, and the angel of the Lord causes Gid's offering of meat and bread to be consumed by fire. This satisfies Gid, at least for a while, though he is amazed that he was able to encounter God face-to-face and yet be permitted to live. But after Gideon assembles his troops, he has doubts again. He wants proof that God will really save Israel by his hand. So he puts a wool fleece on the threshing room floor overnight and tells God that if the dew is only on the fleece and the ground is dry, then he will know the Lord will do what he promised. And, the next morning, that's exactly what happened. Never one to leave well enough alone, Gideon then says to God, "Do not be angry with me. Let me make just one more request. Allow me one more test with the fleece. This time make

> Wrestling with the divine was Moses' way of life.

the fleece dry and the ground covered with dew" (Judges 6:39). Fortunately for Gideon, God goes along with this, too, and Gid's faith is bolstered to the point where he will obey God's further instructions and be victorious over the Midianites with only a handful of soldiers—three hundred, to be exact!

> Sometimes God wrestles with us because it enables us to get the help or assurance from him we need.

Sometimes God deigns to wrestle with us because he knows he will like the result and because it will further his plans. And, thankfully, sometimes he does it because it enables us to get the help or assurance from him we need. It's not just the "spiritual giants" who wrestle with God. People of weak faith, like Gideon, can do so, too.

Jabez "The Pain Man"

When Jabez was born, his mother, who seemed to be oblivious to principles about giving your children healthy self-images, named him "Pain" because "I gave birth to him in pain" (1 Chronicles 4:9). Despite his mother's questionable parenting skills, "Pain" made something out of his life. And he did it by crying out to God, "Oh, that you would bless me and enlarge my territory! Let your hand be with me, and keep me from harm so that I will be free from pain" (4:10). The Bible tells us that God answered his prayer. "Pain" became pain-free all because he refused to accept his circumstances, the label he had been given, and even the future his name seemed to lay out before him, and cried out to God instead.

"Bitter Pill" Naomi

Naomi, whose name means "Pleasant," had a life that was anything but. A famine in the Promised Land forced her family to move to another country, Moab, where her husband and her two sons died. With no means to support herself as a widow in a foreign land, Naomi was forced to return home in a sorry state, where her only hope of surviving would be picking up what harvesters left behind and selling her family's property. Her daughters-in-law want to return with her, but Naomi tells them not to "because the LORD's hand has gone out against me!" (Ruth 1:13).

Yet even though she thinks that God has done her dirt, she still believes in the Lord and wants him to bless her daughters-in-law (Ruth 1:8–9). Daughter-in-law Ruth does go with her, and they shock the town when they return in such an abject state. Naomi even wants to change her name from "Pleasant" to "Bitter" because, she says, "the Almighty has made my life very bitter." The Lord had taken away her fullness and replaced it with emptiness and had afflicted her, bringing her misfortune (Ruth 1:19–21). But even so, her faith in the Lord is evident. She doesn't attribute what has happened to her to chance, or bad magic, or to other malevolent deities. No, this was the Almighty's work, no doubt. All-Stars say, "Though he slay me, yet will I believe in him." Naomi, in fact, still believed the Lord would bless others, even if he had rejected her (Ruth 2:19–20). And she makes an effort to improve her and Ruth's lot in life, perhaps showing that she had wrestled with her view of God and felt that, though he may have afflicted her for a season, he could very well turn things around and begin to bless them instead (Ruth 3). In fact, it was through Naomi's efforts that the Lord worked to bring about blessing—a relative marries Ruth and keeps the property in the family, and Naomi is provided for and gets a grandson, Obed, whose own grandson, by the way, just so happens to be David, Israel's greatest king. And, as the women of the town tell her, loyal Ruth's great love was a tremendous blessing in and of itself (Ruth 4:15). Ruth, who was "better" to her "than seven sons," had always been at her side, so God, in fact, was always blessing Naomi even when all she could see were problems.

Sometimes God has answered me during a wrestling bout over why things were going so badly for me by pointing out that, in the midst of hardship, there were still blessings he was giving me that I was ignoring or taking for granted. God's answer is sometimes to open our eyes to what's already there.

"Silent Momma" Hannah

Hannah was childless during a period in history when such a condition was scandalous. Not only that, but 1 Samuel 1:5 says that it was the Lord who had "closed her womb." (Some would have been tempted to say, "Then I reject the Lord!" but not Hannah, as we shall see.) And every time her family would venture to go to the house of the Lord in Shiloh to worship, Hannah's rival, Peninnah (her husband had two wives), would try hard to get under her skin and set her off. Hannah would be left in tears and unable to eat. Worship was not exactly an uplifting experience for her. One day, at Shiloh, although she was in deep distress, she still prayed to the Lord, even though her troubles all seemed to be connected to him. Like all the truly great All-Stars, Hannah wouldn't loosen her hold on God, no matter what he did. She bargained with the Lord, telling him that if he would give her a son, then she would dedicate that child to the Lord's service, and she reminded God that she was his servant (1 Samuel 1:11).

> Sometimes God points out that, in the midst of hardship, there are blessings we are ignoring or taking for granted.

The priest, Eli, like all the men who just don't get it when it comes to women's concerns, saw her praying silently, misunderstood, and concluded that she was drunk. He chastised her, but she refused to be intimidated by this religious authority figure and explained to him that she was pouring out her soul to the Lord (verse 15). She didn't want her integrity questioned, but wanted it understood that she was suffering "great anguish and grief" (verse 16). Eli then tells her to go in peace and expresses a desire that the Lord would grant her what she asked of him. The Lord does just that, and Hannah keeps her part of the bargain and also offers up a prayer of praise (1 Samuel 2).

Spiritual wrestling champs, like "Silent Momma," are good sports and remember to thank the Lord and to keep their promises. I admit that sometimes I have been so elated when an answer came that I forgot to acknowledge the One who gave it! It's easy to focus on the gift and overlook the giver.

David "Pretty Boy" Jesseson

David, Israel's greatest king, was far from perfect. At one point he shirked his sovereign duty (2 Samuel 11:1) and became a "Peeping Tom" to spy on a bathing beauty (11:2). He then committed adultery with her and, like politicians who have affairs in our day, tried to cover it up. When his plan failed, he had her husband murdered so that he could take her as his wife. They had a son together, yet they didn't live happily ever after. Second Samuel 11:27 ends with the ominous words, "But the thing David had done displeased the LORD."

Sure enough, the prophet Nathan is sent by God to convict "Pretty Boy" of his sin and to tell him of the impending judgments God would execute because of it, including the coming death of his infant son and the revolt of another son, Absalom. The child born because of David's sin became ill, and David began to wrestle with the Lord over his fate. "David pleaded with God for the child. He fasted and went into his house and spent the nights lying on the ground. The elders of his household stood beside him to get him up from the ground, but he refused, and he would not eat any food with them" (2 Samuel 12:16–17). On the seventh day, however, the child died. David "lost," but he accepted this No from God, and then went on with his life, worshiping the Lord once again.

If the "credits" to Psalm 51 are accurate, Dave also wrestled with God during this time period over his own fate. He pled for forgiveness and begged, "Do not cast me from your presence or take your Holy Spirit from me" (Psalm 51:11). This time David won, but, being a father myself, I can't help wondering if he would have rather lost, if that would have meant that his son could live. (See how he responded when Absalom died in 2 Samuel 18:33.)

Elisha "The 'Me Too' Kid"

The Lord was going to take the great prophet Elijah up into heaven. Word of his soon-to-be departure had been given to the prophetic community and his successor/apprentice Elisha knew of it. Because of this, Elisha refused to leave Elijah's side, even though Elijah kept telling him to stay behind. Elisha wanted to inherit a double portion of Elijah's spirit (2 Kings 2:9). Elijah tells "The 'Me Too' Kid" that if Elisha can see him when God takes him away, the double portion will be his; if not, it won't be. Though the Lord had appointed Elisha to be the prophet who would fill Elijah's shoes back in 1 Kings 19:15–21, "The 'Me Too' Kid" was required to make an effort in order for the calling to be fulfilled. He did indeed see Elijah depart this world amidst the chariot and horses of fire and the

> Sometimes we have to cling to what we believe God is calling us to do, despite what others, even godly people, may be telling us to the contrary.

whirlwind and so received his blessing—proving it by parting the waters of the Jordan River (2 Kings 2:13–15).

All-Star wrestlers, like Elisha, know that sometimes in order to receive a blessing they have to cling to what they believe God is calling them to do, despite what others, even godly people, may be telling them to the contrary.

"I'm Not Just a Pop Musician, My Songs Are Full of Theology" Asaph

In Psalm 73, the musician Asaph shows us that he was his generation's Bob Dylan, or Bono (of the rock group U2). Like them, he writes popular songs with "heavy" lyrics. Here, Asaph wrestles with God about why it is that evil people seem to get along just fine in the world and are well rewarded, while he and the righteous experience all sorts of problems and have apparently lived a good life for nothing. He considers the consequences were he to voice his doubts aloud (verse 15) and confesses that the whole question was beyond him (verse 16). Until, that is, he went into the sanctuary (verse 17).

Though champion spiritual wrestlers go through periods of doubt, confusion, and despair, they don't stop clinging to God or exposing themselves to the church, the Word, the sacraments, and the body of Christ, the very means by which they may one day receive answers, comfort, and hope. Asaph's answer was that the prosperity of the unrighteous is only an illusion, a trap that God springs on them so that he may bring judgment against them (verses 18–20). And Asaph realizes that he *is* receiving a reward for his pious living—God himself (verses 23–26)!

Though spiritual wrestlers sometimes don't get the material answers they are trying to obtain, they gain a more intimate relationship with God in the process. And they literally wouldn't trade that for the world!

Jeremiah "Being a Prophet Can Be a Bummer" Hilkiahson

Instead of eagerly embracing the prophet's office as Elisha had done, Jeremiah wrestled with God over: his calling (Jeremiah 1:4–8); the message of doom and judgment by means of a foreign nation that he, who was essentially a patriot, had to deliver (Jeremiah 14:11–22; Lamentations); and the lifelong persecution such a message earned him (Jeremiah 15:10; 17:14–18; 20:7–18), including a trip to the stocks, having his written message burned, hearing death threats, suffering arrest and imprisonment, and being left to die, sinking into the mud at the bottom of an old cistern. He also had to wrestle with God to find the hope that the Jews would ever be able to return to their land after being exiled by the Babylonians (Jeremiah 32).

Through it all, though, Jerry remained faithful to the mission the Lord had given him and was honest in his questions to God and in expressing his reactions and feelings to what was going on— even to the point of uttering words that seem blasphemous to us:

> "Oh, LORD, you deceived me, and I was deceived; you overpowered me and prevailed. . . . So the word of the LORD has brought me insult and reproach all day long. But if I say, 'I will not mention him or speak any more in his name,' his word is in my heart like a fire, a fire shut up in my bones. I am weary of holding it in; indeed, I cannot. . . . Cursed be the day I was born! May the day my mother bore me not be blessed! . . . Why did I ever come out of the womb to see trouble and sorrow and to end my days in shame?" (Jeremiah 20:7, 8–9, 14, 18).

The wrestlers in the Bible were not as repressed as we often are and weren't interested in hiding their true selves from God. They knew it was impossible to do so anyway.

Tag Team — Exiled Israelites "The Aliens"

The Jews truly were strangers in a strange land when they were forced into exile by the Babylonians, and their beloved Jerusalem with its magnificent temple was no more. In psalms, they poured out their sorrow, their confusion, and their deep disappointment. What did it mean to be a Jew when the sacrificial system had ended and the promises of God all seemed to be null and void? How were

> For those who have been through a crisis, often what is believed and what is experienced just don't seem to be one and the same.

they to live in a pagan culture where they didn't belong? "How can we sing the songs of the LORD while in a foreign land?" (Psalm 137:4). Yet, they worked at bolstering their faith and tried to hold on to God despite their bleak predicament (Psalm 137:5–7). They reminded themselves of what God had done in the past while reminding him of what he had pledged. While remembering the Lord, they, nonetheless, honestly acknowledged that their present situation was bleak and asked the Lord to do something before it was too late (Psalm 89).

For those who have been through a crisis, making theological sense of one's situation and matching a hopeful faith to a devastating daily life often involves wrestling. What is believed and what is experienced just don't seem to be one and the same.

"Dan the Man"

The prophet Daniel was one of those who had gone into exile and yet had kept the faith. He wrestled with trying to understand the meanings of the messages God sent him and with their implications for the Lord's people, particularly as these messages involved persecution, political upheaval, and destruction. In his search for understanding, he wasn't afraid to approach heavenly beings and ask for clarification (Daniel 7:15–16), though the answer disturbed him (7:28). Daniel meditated on his visions, trying to comprehend them, even though one of them left him exhausted, ill, and appalled for several days (8:27). Daniel fasted in sackcloth and ashes, seeking the Lord about the end of the desolation of Jerusalem that Jeremiah had prophesied years before. The message he received in response caused him to mourn for three weeks, refusing to pamper himself or eat choice foods (10:2–3). He was so overcome with anguish when another vision came that he had to ask God's messenger for the strength to receive it (10:15–19).

Spiritual wrestling All-Stars grapple with the Word of God, even if it causes injuries. They aren't afraid to ponder what God is telling them, even if the message is painful and hard to accept. Such grappling often leads to even more wrestling, as new insights come and more questions arise.

I always shake my head when I hear someone criticize Christianity as "a crutch" that people lean on in order to be promised pie-in-the-sky by and by. Christianity, rather than plying me with platitudes, has given me plenty of messages that I find extremely hard to swallow. Some can even make me sick if I dwell on them, as Daniel's messages did for him. For example, Christianity tells me that some of my friends and relatives will be cast into hell forever. Christianity informs me that there are powerful spiritual forces that oppose me, bent on my destruction. Christianity teaches that God sometimes allows his people to be tortured and to die horrible deaths, as some of my brothers and sisters are experiencing around the globe even as I write these words. I embrace Christianity because it is true, not because it's always soothing or palatable.

"Joyless" Job

The children of Israel deserved the anguish they experienced during their exile because they had broken their covenant with God, but there was a character in the Old Testament who didn't deserve any of the horrible things that happened to him. Job was God's favorite person out of all who lived on the earth, was scrupulously pious, and possessed a heart-felt faith. But, because of what was taking place in heaven between God and Satan, Job lost his children, his wealth, his health, and, due to the common assumption that if something bad happened to you it was because you had sinned, his good name and his standing in the community.

Job, being the fighter that he was, didn't take all this lying down. Throughout the book that bears his name, he argues against his friends who endlessly repeat the orthodox party line of their day, namely that Job must repent of his great sins if he ever wants to be blessed by God again. The friends purport to be relaying God's truth, yet Job fights against their assertions. Job knows that he isn't being punished for anything he's done and proceeds to give evidence that the world doesn't work according to a system of rewards and penalties. Job also keeps calling out to God, demanding a fair hearing before him. And Job wrestles with his view of God, trying hard to maintain trust in the Lord and to affirm God's good character, but at the same time feeling as though the King of the universe has arbitrarily decided to target him and that there's absolutely nothing that Job, a mere mortal, can do about it. Like Job, spiritual wrestlers dare to grapple with beliefs and assumptions, even those considered true and acceptable by the religious establishment. And wrestlers don't take what's happening to them lying down, but cry out to God continually, as Job did.

Job finally gets his requested audience with God in chapters 38–41, but the Lord never really addresses Job's specific situation nor answers his questions. God essentially says, "I'm much bigger and wiser than you and, therefore, you can't accuse me of anything." Though Job still doesn't know how to reconcile what happened to him with the idea of a just God, he has seen the Lord in all his divine glory and power and, for him, that's enough (Job 42:5). Job came to the same conclusion that so many of us wrestlers have come to, that, pertaining to the ways and the mind of an infinite God, there will always be things we do not understand, "things too wonderful for me to know" (Job 42:3). Job's friends are condemned because they arrogantly assumed they had God and the world all figured out and thus had inadvertently lied about the Lord (Job 42:7–8).

All-Star wrestlers are wary of teammates or coaches who seem to have all the easy answers. Watch out for people who know exactly why God is allowing bad things to happen to you and what he's trying to teach you through them, or who see no gray areas in Christian doctrine or conduct, or who act horrified at the thought that real Christians sometimes have questions!

> Watch out for people who know exactly why God is allowing bad things to happen to you and what he's trying to teach you through them.

"The Pugnacious Preacher"

The books of Job and Ecclesiastes could be titled "The Anti-Proverbs Books," because, whereas the book of Proverbs (and many psalms) would say that the righteous and the wise are blessed out of their socks in this life, Job and Ecclesiastes reply, "Wanna bet?" Or maybe it's more accurate to call Job and Ecclesiastes "Books That Balance Out Proverbs (and many of the psalms)." Taken all together, the books biblical scholars refer to as

"Wisdom Literature"—Psalms, Proverbs, Ecclesiastes, Song of Songs—paint us a realistic picture of life with all of its extremes. Yes, many times the godly are blessed, but many times they aren't.

The writer of Ecclesiastes, who was a teacher and perhaps the leader of an assembly (that's why I call him a preacher), was determined to use his brain and examine life as it truly was here on earth. He discovers that living for pleasure, wisdom, and one's work are all ultimately meaningless, unfulfilling, and pointless. "So far, so good," we Christians would say. "He's right on the money." But in his ruthless examination of life as it exists on our planet, he saw oppression without relief (Ecclesiastes 4:1–3); God's blessing of a man, but not giving him the ability to enjoy the blessings (Ecclesiastes 6:1–6); God bringing good and evil to people, seemingly without any reason (7:13–14; 8:16–17; 9:11–12; 10:8–9); righteous people suffering and wicked people prospering (7:15; 8:14); foolish men being put in leadership roles (10:5–7); and many among the elderly who could hardly call old age and long life "a blessing" (Ecclesiastes 12:1–5). His conclusion that everything is "meaningless" is hardly one we would embrace, yet we can easily see how he arrived at it.

While it is true that other parts of the Scripture answer some of the author's concerns, it's also interesting to note that God included this book, as it is, in the Bible—questions, contradictions, wrestling moments, and all. Once again the point is made that God's All-Star Team consists of those who face life as it truly is without trying to sugarcoat everything or ignoring the difficulties that may arise with one's faith because of an honest examination or inquiry. God is the God of truth, not half-truths, fantasies, or wishful thinking.

Next, we'll look at the All-Star Team from that other, though related, wrestling federation, the New Testament.

It's Your Turn

Here are some questions to stimulate your own thoughts as you interact with this chapter.

(*Note:* Groups may want to use two or more sessions to discuss the chapter.)

1. Which of the biblical All-Stars can you relate to, and why?

2. Which of the biblical All-Stars is the most unlike you, and why?

3. How would you answer someone who says, "The Old Testament is irrelevant because we live under the new covenant?"

4. Are you as honest with God as you'd like to be? If so, is that a good thing? If not, what hinders you?

"Awesome" Abraham

5. What do our prayers accomplish? Can we really change God's mind about anything?

6. Why do some of the All-Stars preface their requests to God with, "Now, don't get angry"? Have you ever prayed prayers that you feared would anger God? Were you right to pray them or not?

"Gorgeous Jake"

7. Has God ever been at work answering your prayers and concerns as you used your common sense and your own resources? If you're in a group, can you tell the other members about it? When did you recognize that God was behind it all?

8. What do you make of the fact that God was intending to kill Moses and, later, the children of Israel? What can the accounts of these events mean to us who live in the Christian Era?

Gideon "You Must Be Joking" Joashson

9. Is it wrong for us to put our own "fleeces" before the Lord or ask him for signs? Have you ever done so? What was the result?

Tag Team—Exiled Israelites "The Aliens"

10. Have you ever felt that you were in a "strange land" where it was hard to hang on to God? What did you do? Maybe you face such a situation every day at work, or in school, or at home. What do you do?

"Dan the Man"

11. Has a message from God or a truth about him, the world, or the Christian life ever disturbed you? If you're in a group, can you tell the members about it?

"Joyless" Job and "The Pugnacious Preacher"

12. Was there ever a time when well-meaning, even godly, people gave you bad advice or wrong teachings? How did you know it was bad or wrong? What did you do about it? How did you feel toward them?

13. In what ways can a person who quotes prooftexts and standard religious answers learned in Sunday school be pleasing to God? In what ways can a different person who refuses to prooftext and questions the standard answers also be pleasing to God?

14. As you look at the world and at your own life and the lives of those you know, do you see some things happening that are hard to reconcile with the beliefs of the Christian faith? How do you handle those things?

15. Are there any questions or concerns you have after reading this chapter?

Chapter 7

The New Testament All-Star Team

I've given the New Testament its own wing in my "Spiritual Wrestling Hall of Fame." A quick tour through it, becoming acquainted with some of the inductees, will give us yet more helpful insights on wrestling with God. It will also help us to see that "there's nothing new under the sun." The matches we have with the Almighty are similar to those our spiritual ancestors had. Let's meet the wrestlers!

Jesus "The Messiah" Josephson

Examining the life of our Lord and Savior gives us an opportunity to observe both how a human wrestles with God and how God wrestles with mankind. After all, Jesus was both God and man.

As a man, a young man at the tender age of twelve actually, Jesus wrestled with the Scriptures, the religious leaders, and the theological positions of his day, viewing this as the most important thing he had to do. Jesus was amazed that his parents didn't seem to understand his strong motivation (Luke 2:41–50).

As a pastor, I sadly shake my head over the large number of teenagers who have grown up in churches but are biblically illiterate. How many young people today in the twenty-first century believe that delving into the Bible and exploring theological truth are the things they *have* to do? Instead, it's, "*I have* to go to the mall," or "*I have* to get to basketball practice." Yeah, teenagers today, what can you do with them? But before we get too down on the kids, let's ask how many adults *have* to be in their Father's house? And how many adults would think it was healthy if their kids *did* spend much of their time centered on the things of God? ("You need to get outside and play more! Why don't you join the soccer team?") Spiritual All-Stars like Jesus are those for whom the pursuit of God and his truth is a burning passion all the time.

In Gethsemane, an older Jesus wrestled with God's plan for his life. The Father loved Jesus and had a wonderful plan. However, that wonderful plan entailed Jesus first being publicly humiliated, branded as a criminal, and tortured to death, before he received the victor's crown on the throne in glory. Though throughout his ministry Jesus had resolutely and unswervingly faced this fact, and had even seemingly gone out of his way to provoke the authorities to get them to crucify him, he was a real flesh-and-blood human being. As such, on the night he was to be betrayed and arrested, "he began to be sorrowful and troubled" and "overwhelmed . . . to the point of death" (Matthew 26:37–38). Three times he pleaded with God that, if it were possible, he could be spared the gruesome parts of the plan. But he also added that he wanted to see the Father's will, and not his own, done. All-Stars know that often God's productive plans involve pain. And they are not afraid to tell God that they don't much like it and would rather be spared the hurt. They ask God if there might not be a "Plan B" or even a "Plan C" that would be easier. But, in the end, they are willing to submit to God, acknowledging that his ways are the best and that the good that will be accomplished through the plan is worth the pain they must go through.

Hanging on the cross for three hours in physical and spiritual agony, Jesus exhibited the tenacity that all the great ones have. Even as he felt totally forsaken by the Father, he still called out to God and asked for an answer (Matthew 27:46). Wrestlers cling to God, holding on by faith, no matter what happens to them. They won't release their grip on God, even if it seems, at times, as though God has released his grip on them. They will keep trying to pin God to the mat and receive answers, blessings, or a renewed sense of his presence, even when it appears that he's doing his best to slip away.

> In the end, All-Stars are willing to submit to God, acknowledging that his ways are the best and that the good that will be accomplished through the plan is worth the pain they must go through.

Which brings me to a consideration of how Jesus taught about and demonstrated the ways God wrestles with humans. I've already said quite a bit about Jesus playing forms of "hide-and-seek" with people in chapter 2, so here I'll concentrate on how the Father and the Son seemingly try to escape when people are attempting to pin them down.

Jesus told two parables about persistent prayers that have always bugged me. In fact, the parables themselves deal with "bugging." In one, a widow keeps bugging an unjust judge until she finally wears him down and he rules in her favor just to shut her up and make her go away (Luke 18:1–7). In the other, found in Luke 11:5–13, a friend bugs another friend at midnight, asking for a favor. The other friend won't get up and take action for friendship's sake. (I know how he felt. I don't much like late-night calls, either!) Depending on how verse 8 is translated, he will finally get up and get moving either because of his friend's persistence or because of his boldness. At any rate, the impression given is that the one with the bread takes action because he wants to go back to bed and wants his family to get some peace, not because of any noble motives. The point that Jesus makes in these parables is that if we can even get humans who are disinclined to lift a finger on our behalf to eventually do our will just by continually irritating them, how much more can we get a loving heavenly Father to answer our requests by continually bringing those requests to him. Luke said that Jesus was showing the disciples, through this parable, that they ought to pray and never give up (18:1). However, Jesus tacitly acknowledges the possibility that Christians may be tempted to believe that God won't help them because answers aren't always forthcoming (18:8).

My question here is "Why?" Why that temptation, if, indeed, God will see that his people get justice "quickly" (18:8)? Why aren't answers always forthcoming? Why should needy children have to ask an all-powerful, all-loving Father for anything more than once? It always seemed to me that Jesus, while wanting to contrast God with the amoral judge and the awakened and annoyed friend, actually wound up inadvertently teaching that, in one way, God is exactly the same as them. He won't respond unless you keep after him.

But, of course, Jesus never does anything inadvertently. I've come to see that these parables have a secondary purpose beyond urging us to persevere in prayer. They reveal to us a part of what is the nature of the relationship between God and man—namely, that God will sometimes act as if he's blowing you off when you come to him in prayer. Haven't you ever felt that your prayers were being ignored by God? That they were just bouncing off the ceiling and the walls, accomplishing nothing? Only if you keep pestering

God, believing that he's the only One able to help and there's no place else to turn, will anything get done eventually.

The difference between God and the reluctant characters in the parables is that, while the judge withheld justice because he "neither feared God nor cared about man" (18:2), and while the friend initially told his buddy to honor the "Do Not Disturb" sign hanging on his door because he and his family were bedded down for the night, God with-

> God withholds instant answers out of nobler motives. He may want to impress upon us that he is really the One in charge.

holds instant answers out of nobler motives. He may want to impress upon us that he is really the One in charge and that he's not a genie who will do our bidding at the snap of our fingers or the rubbing of a lamp. You see, God is more interested in our hearts, so he may want to test, or refine, or strengthen, or draw out our faith. He may just want to see what we'll come up with to try to get through to him. As I have said before, he wants to have an ongoing, interactive relationship with us, not a superficial one.

Jesus, as God's perfect representative, demonstrated in his earthly ministry the prerogative of God to occasionally delay granting our requests in order to engage in some sparring with us. Consider the following instances where Jesus' initial response to people was "Get lost":

- Jesus seems, at first, to snub his own mother in John 2:1–11! They are attending a wedding when Mary points out to Jesus that the host's wine has run out. His response is, "Dear woman, why do you involve me? My time has not yet come." But Mary, showing her own style of tenacity, and that she deserves a place in my "Hall of Fame" (see the next section), evidently believes that Jesus will eventually respond, and so she tells the servants to do whatever Jesus tells them. Sure enough, Jesus turns water into wine—lots of it! And it was the good stuff, too!

- After the disciples had returned from their missionary journey and were debriefing with Jesus, so many people were milling around them that they didn't even have a chance to eat or to catch their breath. Jesus wanted to take them away to a place where they could rest. His reaction to the hustle and bustle was "Come on, guys, let's get out of here." They left the questing crowd behind and sailed to what they hoped would be a secluded spot, but the crowd saw where they were heading and ran around the body of water, beating them to their destination. Then, instead of trying yet another spot, Jesus had compassion on the crowd and ministered to them. (See Mark 6:30–44.)

- Matthew 15:21–28 and Mark 7:24–30 tell the story of some-one who had two strikes against her when she requested that Jesus deliver her daughter from demon possession. First, she was a woman, and second, she was a Gentile. But, of course, compassionate Jesus, the One who broke through cultural barriers and hated stereotypes, instantly reached out to her in love, didn't he? Not exactly. Actually, at first he treated her like pond scum! He totally ignored her and then, when she wouldn't go away or shut up, he said that he only came to minister to the lost sheep of Israel. He told her that it wasn't right to take bread that was meant for the children (the Jews) and toss it to their dogs (the Gentiles)! But she retorted that even the dogs can have the crumbs that fall off the family's table. Jesus then granted her request. Matthew says that Jesus commended her highly for her great faith. Mark seems to add another slant to the healing by recording that Jesus told her, "For such a reply, you may go; the demon has left your daughter" (Mark 7:29). In other words, Jesus might have been saying, "That was a good one! Pretty cool! I enjoyed that witty, wise comeback!"

- When word is sent to Jesus that one of his best friends, Lazarus, is sick, he takes no action for three days. When he finally goes to Lazarus' house, it seems as if he's too late. Lazarus is already dead. Laz's sisters, Martha and Mary, and the mourners can't understand why Jesus delayed. Surely he could have come and healed his friend, and a death could have been prevented! But through some give-and-take with Martha, Jesus makes it clear to her that all hope has not been lost. And when he asks that the stone be removed from the entrance to Lazarus' tomb, Martha (though she at first protests) accepts Jesus' word that if she believes she will see the glory of God. Then she allows the tomb to be opened. Talk about faith! You go, Girl! (Incidentally, I've nominated Martha and Mary for my "Hall of Fame," too, both for this bout and also for the one recorded in Luke 10:38–42. There Mary sat at Jesus' feet to soak up his teaching, though women weren't supposed to do so in that day and age. And when Martha had a complaint about it, she didn't hold it in, but took it right to the Lord. These sisters are sure bets to be inducted one of these years.) In Lazarus' case, Jesus chose to purposely delay. Though he was ultimately going to heal his friend, it wasn't in the way everyone at first had thought. God's purpose was that the disciples' faith would be strengthened, probably for the upcoming crucifixion and Christ's own resurrection. You can read the whole story in John 11:1–44.

- We last visited the road to Emmaus in chapter 2, but we need to revisit it briefly now. Jesus appeared there "undercover" to two of his disciples who didn't recognize him. However, he did explain to them the scriptural solution to the mystery of what had become of the Messiah. And when they were approaching the village where the disciples were headed, "Jesus acted as if he were going farther" (Luke 24:28). But, the disciples, in Luke's words, "urged him strongly" (v. 29) to stay with them. Later, as they were all eating the evening meal, Jesus opened their eyes and revealed to the disciples that he was indeed the One they had seen crucified, but was now risen. So, to recap, Jesus, though teaching the disciples and blessing them, but not yet fully disclosing himself to them, acted as though it was his intention to leave them. It was only after some strong urging on their part that he agreed to stay. I wonder what would have happened if they hadn't tried hard to get him to stay. Would Christ have simply just moved on, leaving the disciples forever in the dark as to who he really was?

Championship level wrestlers know that they must keep on keeping on with God, no matter how hard it may appear he is trying to draw away. Once they get a hold of him, they never let him escape. And he, in turn, honors their efforts.

Mary "The Blessed"

When the angel Gabriel appeared to Mary (the young woman who would be Jesus' mother) and called her a "highly favored" one and told her that the Lord was with her, Mary was "greatly troubled at his words and wondered what kind of greeting this might be" (Luke 1:28–29). All-Stars are always humble, knowing that, compared to God, they are nothing and don't deserve accolades. After Gabriel tells her that she will become pregnant, Mary is bold enough, or perhaps desperate or confused enough, to question him about how this will be, since she is a virgin. Gabriel answers her honest question, and then Mary humbly accepts God's will, allowing him to overpower and change her life in a way no woman had before or since. Later, when Jesus was born and the shepherds had their strange experience, "Mary treasured up all these things and pondered them in her heart" (Luke 2:19). Mary, like the All-Star she is, practiced the fundamentals—storing up God's truths, meditating on them, and asking questions about them. Mary didn't always

> Mary, like the All-Star she is, practiced the fundamentals—storing up God's truths, meditating on them, and asking questions about them.

quite understand what her son was all about. We surmise that at one point she was one of several family members thinking he was out of his mind and wanting to "take charge of him" (Mark 3:21). In other words, she wanted to take him away and have him watched closely and basically "sat on," lest he hurt himself or others. But she didn't spurn him. She appeared at the foot of Jesus' cross with the apostle John (John 19:25–27), while some others who had followed him stood off at a distance (Luke 23:49).

Tag Team—The Jerusalem Church— "Peter's Persistent Prayer Posse"

The early Christians were going through a hard time. Herod had arrested some of them and had executed James, the brother of John. Now another apostle, Peter, had been imprisoned, awaiting a "trial" (in other words, his own execution). However, the church "was earnestly praying to God for him" (Acts 12:5). Even though it could have meant more arrests if the authorities knew what they were doing, and though Herod had shown his "power" by having one of the leaders of the people of God put to death by the sword, the Christians still kept right on meeting together, asking God to intervene and free Peter. In fact, on the very night before Peter's "trial" (Acts 12:6), when we might expect believers to throw in the towel because all hope would have seemed to be gone, many of them were gathered at a home, praying. Like the All-Stars they were, the members of the Jerusalem church intended to pray right up until even the last minute. Until it became evident that God was really answering No, they would keep on praying. But, in this case, God answered Yes and Peter was miraculously released and made his way to the house. He didn't suspect that God was about to totally floor the praying Christians. When Peter knocked at their door, a servant girl recognized his voice and joyfully announced that Peter was outside. And the Christians welcomed him in, praised God, and embraced him—NOT! Instead, they told the servant, "You're out of your mind" (12:15). She kept insisting, so this time the prayer partners reasoned, "It must be his angel." The idea that God may have actually heard their prayers and delivered Peter to them never seemed to have entered their minds. Peter kept right on knocking, and finally they opened the door and "were astonished" (12:16). God had pinned them right to the mat with that move! And all he had to do was grant their request!

Paul "The Epistler"

I've already talked in chapter 2 about how God kept putting the moves on Saul, the persecutor of the early church, until the Lord finally stopped holding back and pinned Saul down once and for all. But the converted Saul (called Paul) wrestled with God again.

In fact, 2 Corinthians 12:1–10 tells us of the time God and Satan teamed up to take on Paul! This hardly seems fair, does it? Wrestling with just one of these formidable "mat men" would be challenging enough, but both at once?! Actually, though, Paul pretty much ignores Satan beyond just noting he is involved. Paul concentrates all of his energies on God, knowing that he is the team Captain/Coach. God was the One who was really calling the shots and was totally in control, using the ill wind that Satan was blowing into Paul's life to ultimately accomplish something needful and good.

It all went down like this:

Paul had been taken by God up to the third heaven and, in paradise, "heard inexpressible things, things that man is not permitted to tell" (2 Corinthians 12:4). However, in conjunction with this trip (or maybe it was a vision), Paul received, in his words, "a thorn in my flesh, a messenger of Satan, to torment me" (12:7). Many have speculated on what this "thorn" was—a persecutor, an eye disease, stage fright, persistent sexual temptation—but it really doesn't matter for our purposes. What's important is what Paul did about it. Though the thorn was the means God used to keep Paul from becoming conceited (because, after all, he had been to heaven and back and was made privy to the secrets of the Lord), Paul still didn't like it very much. So, rather than just resignedly accepting what was happening to him as "God's will," he did what an All-Star would do. He pleaded with the Lord, not once, but three times to have the thorn taken away from him (v. 8). But the Lord won those matches, refusing to remove the thorn but also telling Paul, "My grace is sufficient for you, for my power is made perfect in weakness" (v. 9). Paul accepted "defeat" and even saw the benefit of continuing to live with the thorn. It would make him rely on the power of Christ to overcome his weakness. He even got to the point where he would boast about, and delight in, his troubles (vv. 9–10)!

The truly great wrestlers know that bringing their feelings, concerns, and desires honestly to God enables interaction to take place so that, even if the match turns out differently than they would have liked, something productive can still come from it.

> The truly great wrestlers know that bringing their feelings, concerns, and desires honestly to God enables interaction to take place so that something productive can still come from the contest.

Earlier in that same letter, Paul had talked about his weakness and described what many wrestlers down through the ages have felt like as they have held on tight to God through hard times:

> But we have this treasure in jars of clay to show that this all-surpassing power is from God and not from us. We are hard pressed on every side, but not crushed; perplexed, but not in despair; persecuted, but not abandoned; struck down, but not destroyed. We always carry around in our body the death of Jesus, so that the life of Jesus may also be revealed in our body (2 Corinthians 4:7–10).

Chapters 20 and 21 of Acts give the play-by-play account of another of Paul's matches with God. In chapter 20, Paul tells the elders of the church in Ephesus, "And now, compelled by the Spirit, I am going to Jerusalem, not knowing what will happen to me there. I only know that in every city the Holy Spirit warns me that prison and hardships are facing me" (vv. 22–23). Notice that the Spirit is leading Paul to Jerusalem, yet cautioning him about the dangers that lie ahead. Perhaps the Holy Spirit just wanted Paul to be prepared and not be taken by surprise when the persecution came, or not to feel that God had been taken by surprise either. Or perhaps the Spirit was testing Paul to see if he could be dissuaded from his divine mission. Would Paul hold on to his mission, and thus on to God's will for his life, and ultimately on to God himself? Or would he allow the Spirit to throw him off? This certainly seems to be the Spirit's intent in chapter 21. As Paul is on his way to Jerusalem, he stays with the disciples living at Tyre for seven days. Luke writes, "Through the Spirit they urged Paul not to go on to Jerusalem" (v. 4). Did you catch that? The Spirit is now urging Paul to give up his mission! Then when Paul and his traveling companions reach Caesarea, a prophet named Agabus comes down from Judea. He takes Paul's belt, ties his own hands and feet with it, saying, "The Holy Spirit says, 'In this way the Jews of Jerusalem will bind the owner of this belt and will hand him over to the Gentiles'" (v. 11). Then Paul's companions and the Christians there plead with Paul not to go. So the body of Christ is now telling Paul to stay away from Jerusalem. They must have interpreted the prophecy as a sort of "Keep Out of Jerusalem" sign. But Paul tells them, "I am ready not only to be bound, but also to die in Jerusalem for the name of the Lord Jesus" (v. 13). When Paul won't be dissuaded, the church gives up, saying, "The Lord's will be done" (v. 14). Huh? Now the Christians feel as though it is God's will that Paul goes to Jerusalem and suffers, whereas just a little while ago they obviously thought God was warning Paul to stay away? Paul's determination seems to have won them over. While the prophecy aspects of Acts 21 and 22 are difficult to understand and have caused endless debates, I think that part of the Caesarean church's change in attitude is that they came to share what must have been Paul's viewpoint all along. The prophecies weren't prohibitions, but tests. They were the means by which the Holy Spirit wrestled with Paul.

Tag Team — The Martyrs of the Book of Hebrews "Take a Lickin' and Keep Right on Tickin'"

Some of the people talked about in Hebrews chapter 11 have actually been inducted into two "Halls of Fame." They made the biblical author's cut of those who should be in the "Faith Hall of Fame," and they are also members of my "Spiritual Wrestling Hall of Fame."

> Some biblical saints who lived all their earthly lives without ever having received what had been promised must have done some intense wrestling with God.

After the author of Hebrews talks about people who were literally able to work miracles because of their faith, and who escaped certain death, and who changed the world, he goes on to a different set of saints:

Others were tortured and refused to be released, so that they might gain a better resurrection. Some faced jeers and flogging, while still others were chained and put in prison. They were stoned; they were sawed in two; they were put to death by the sword. They went about in sheep-skins and goatskins, destitute, persecuted and mistreated—the world was not worthy of them. They wandered in deserts and mountains, and in caves and holes in the ground. These were all commended for their faith, yet none of them received what had been promised (vv. 35b–39).

Surely these people who lived all their earthly lives without ever having received what had been promised must have done some intense wrestling with God! Especially since they clung to their faith, and therefore to their God, throughout extremely hard times.

Tag Team — The Martyrs of the Book of Revelation — "The Noisy Ones"

The apostle John was caught up to the heavenly realm in a vision. He writes in Revelation 6:9–11, "I saw under the altar the souls of those who had been slain because of the word of God and the testimony they had maintained. They called out in a loud voice,

'How long, Sovereign Lord, holy and true, until you judge the inhabitants of the earth and avenge our blood?' Then each of them was given a white robe, and they were told to wait a little longer, until the number of their fellow servants and brothers who were to be killed as they had been was completed."

You gotta love these guys! Here they are in heaven, enjoying a blessed state (Revelation 14:13), and yet they still shout out a question to God. They are my kind of people! They're not going to let a little thing like being dead prevent them from wrestling with God! They are still trying to figure out God and his mysterious ways. They still have concerns that haven't yet been dealt with. And they have no intention of letting sleeping dogs lie. Wrestlers to the end—and beyond! No wonder they are in the "Hall of Fame!"

Next, we will look more closely at the moves and holds involved in wrestling with God and find out what these may look like in our modern world.

It's Your Turn

Here are some questions to stimulate your own thoughts as you interact with this chapter, either by yourself or in a group.

1. Has there ever been a time when you felt as though God were trying to give you "the brush off," or escape from you as you prayed? What did you do about it? How did the match end? If you've never had that experience, what might it be like for you if you did?

2. Was there ever a painful part of God's will that you had to submit to? Do you see the divine wisdom behind it now or not?

3. How can you store up the truths in the Bible and what God has done in your life and ponder them in your heart?

4. Have you ever been utterly amazed by an answer to prayer? Maybe even a little embarrassed by it because at some level in your heart, you really didn't think that God would come through?

5. Can you think of a time when God's grace and power shone through your weakness? If you're in a group, would you share about it?

6. Why does God rescue some of his people from prison and death and yet allow others of them to suffer and be executed?

7. Are there any questions or concerns you have after reading this chapter?

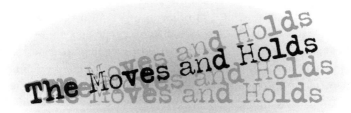

Chapter 8

The Moves and Holds

The objective of any sport is pretty simple when you come right down to it. In golf, you're supposed to get the little ball in the little cup using the least number of strokes. In baseball, your team has to get more of your people to cross home plate than the other team does. In basketball, the objective is to put the ball through the hoop more times than the other team can. It's in the accomplishing of all these seemingly uncomplicated tasks that the skill and strategy come into play.

This is a fact made evident to me whenever I challenge my son and my daughter to a game of hoops. Soon my protesting body, rebelling against performing moves it hasn't practiced in decades, reminds me that basketball is much more complicated than it appears. Not to mention that my long-range jumper of twenty years ago is pretty rusty. My kids have the skill and strategy necessary to compete. To me, though, the simple task is much more complicated than it used to be.

As with basketball, the objective in wrestling sounds simple enough. You're supposed to grab your opponent, hanging on no matter what, and control him or her so that he or she can't move.

And when your opponent, likewise, tries to immobilize you, your job is to break free. But in order to accomplish these simply described objectives, you need to master and practice some basic moves and holds, particularly when you are going up against an opponent as formidable as God. So let's describe and examine those moves and holds as they apply to our objectives—hanging on to God, "controlling" him, and escaping when it looks as though he has you right where he wants you.

Hanging On to God

As we have seen, God will sometimes act as though he is trying to escape from you, or as though he has already accomplished that and is now a million miles away. Sometimes, God doesn't even need to work all that hard at slipping from our grasp. Sometimes, because we don't understand the fundamentals of spiritual wrestling, we just relax our grip, not realizing the consequences of doing so. If we're going to hang on to our wily, slippery, in motion opponent, we will need to master some moves and holds.

Move #1: Continually Entering and Reentering the Ring

It seems as though it should be obvious that if you are trying to hold on to God, especially in the midst of tough or confusing situations, you should keep on going to worship services, Bible studies, small groups, etc., but it's not. Hebrews 10:25 had to urge, "Let us not give up meeting together, as some are in the habit of doing." So, evidently, some of those living back when Hebrews was written were in the habit of skipping out of Christian gatherings. It's an easy habit to fall into today, too. Let's say you're having doubts and really struggling in your day-to-day living as a Christian, so you tell yourself that you haven't done "good enough" during the week to go to church on Sunday, or that you don't feel "joyful enough" to attend. (And, unfortunately, there are some congregations that make it their mission to ensure that only those "good enough," or "joyful enough," or "spiritual enough" feel comfortable among them.) Or you're sure you'd feel like a hypocrite attending any Christian gathering. After all, you're angry with God, so how can you praise and thank him? Or you don't feel as though being involved in a church is doing you any good at the present time. Or you have a thousand and one other excuses that sound valid to you, especially when you're spiritually floundering. The upshot is that you stay away from God's people and the places they frequent. It seems like the reasonable and even "honest" thing to do. I know because I've been there. But let's look at things from a WWF-type of perspective.

Imagine that Muscles McGerk (remember him?) has been doing you dirt. You thought he was your friend, but now you've heard that he's been bad-mouthing you all over town. You wonder if it's true. He never returns your phone calls and always seems to be conveniently absent when you show up at the training gym. You tell your other friends that you'd like to know just what in the world is going on. They convey to you that Muscles says he will only answer you if you can beat

> How can we pick fights with God if we don't go to where he hangs out?

him in a steel cage match next Thursday night. He wonders if you really have it in you to get him to talk. So Thursday night arrives. Muscles has climbed into the steel cage down at the arena and you . . . stay at home napping?! After Muscles gets tired of waiting for you, he goes down to the local bar and grill for some suds and steak. You hear where he is and immediately hop in your car . . . and go catch a late movie?! The next day you are walking past his house and see his car in the driveway. He's there! Now is the time for action, so you . . . head to the mall to do some shopping to cheer you up?! What's wrong with this picture? If you really want answers, or to get Muscles to cease and desist, or even to get some sort of justice for what he's put you through, don't you go where he is and confront him?

How can we pick fights with God if we don't go to where he hangs out? Jesus told us he'd be found hanging out where two or three (or more) come together in his name (Matthew 18:20). And, in Revelation 1:20–2:1, he says that he walks among the congregations. So if you think that maybe your supposed friend, God, may be doing you dirt, or wonder why he's acting strangely or giving you mixed signals, or if you need answers, acknowledgment, and maybe even justice, well, you know where God will be. Go and see what he has to say for himself as he speaks through his servants (Acts 2:16–18; 1 Peter 4:11). Remember that it was after Asaph entered the sanctuary that he received the answer to the question he was wrestling with God over (Psalm 73:16–17).

I have known believers from congregations I've pastored, or been a member of, over the years who kept right on coming to worship services and Bible studies while a loved one was dying a slow and horrible death, or after a family member perished in a car accident, or as a messy divorce was dragging its way through the courts. The believers would sometimes admit that they were feeling pretty lousy and would make counseling appointments with me. They would tell their friends that they were having a hard time believing in God anymore, or couldn't see his hand anywhere, or were downright angry at him. But they kept coming out. And the Lord, as a result, somehow kept sustaining them through weeks, months, or even years of crises because they hung in there despite everything.

Someone has said that a large percentage of winning a battle is just showing up. And he or she was right, particularly when it comes to wrestling with God. So go! Go whether you feel like it or not, whether you have the "right" attitude or not! Go and confront God and let him confront you! Go and keep going!

The Moves and Holds

Move #2: Keep Staring God in the Face

If you want to keep hanging on to God, you've got to stay focused. But we are so easily distracted in our modern, fast-paced world. Sometimes we forget who it is we are grappling with, or even that we're wrestling with a supernatural being at all! Then we loosen our grips, let down our guards, and, whoops, God is gone!

You've probably heard these kinds of expressions: "Nothing has ever gone my way"; "I'm just having a string of bad luck lately"; "Disasters always come in threes"; "That's the way the world is, so what can you do about it"; "I was born under a black cloud"; "Everyone else always gets all the breaks." People, even Christians, make these negative statements about life all the time. But the implication behind these sayings is that we are the victims of some sort of impersonal fate, or of cosmic forces, or of engines of change, and that we are helpless. Helpless? Nothing we can do about it? Don't we have access to the Almighty, miracle-working God who has pledged to love us forever? Rather than moaning about our bad luck, shouldn't we be storming his throne room with our requests? Shouldn't we wrestle with God until either he changes us or our circumstances? And when he does, shouldn't we be like that one lone leper who came back and kneeled at Jesus' feet and thanked him for what he had done?

After all, everything that's happened to you happened because God allowed it to happen, perhaps just as part of the natural consequences of your actions and decisions, or of the consequences of living in a fallen world, or because you were being allowed the privilege of suffering for Christ, or he was disciplining you or testing you or teaching you to mold you into the image of Christ (Romans 8:28–30), or for his own unrevealed reasons. At any point, he could have changed your circumstances either by working a miracle or two, or by influencing events and people, or (for the quantum physicists among my readers) by allowing reality to follow a different course, but he didn't and hasn't—at least not yet. How that corresponds to his love for you is something you'll have to wrestle with him over. But it is him you have to deal with. He is the One ultimately responsible.

Speaking of the one ultimately responsible, I've also heard Christians say (and have said myself) things like: "Satan has really been oppressing me lately"; "I feel like this time the Devil is out to put me away for good"; "The demons are using me for target practice"; "I'm in the midst of spiritual warfare with the Enemy and I'm losing." While these statements may be true and usually are followed with, "So pray for me," we often, in our daily conversations and in our thoughts, concentrate so much on Satan and what he and his minions are allegedly doing that God seems like an afterthought. And a weak one at that. Once again, the idea either intentionally or subtly and unintentionally conveyed is that we are being helplessly overwhelmed by a force more powerful than ourselves, and that there's not a thing we can do about it. Biblically speaking, nothing could be further from the truth. See 1 Corinthians 10:13 (and notice that it says that *God* won't let you be tempted beyond a certain point), James 4:7, and 1 Peter 5:8–11.

> Often, in our daily conversations and in our thoughts, we concentrate so much on Satan and what he and his minions are allegedly doing that God seems like an afterthought.

There is Someone who can turn off the temptations, trials, and persecutions in a split second if he chooses to, and that Someone is God, not Satan. I suspect if it were up to Satan, he'd keep the pressure on continuously, and we'd never get any relief. But the point is that it's not up to Satan. God is the One ultimately in control, and so he's the One we ultimately have to deal with. He is the One ultimately responsible. The buck stops with him. Not that he is the author of evil, or tempts anyone, or ever acts maliciously toward his children, but he is so powerful that he can even use the morally reprehensible and culpable acts that demons and men do to accomplish his sovereign purposes. The cross of Jesus Christ proves that, doesn't it? God can use his enemies as unwitting and unwilling pawns.

And we do not have two equally powerful gods vying for control of the universe—Satan and the Lord. Satan can only go as far as God, in his infinite wisdom and mercy (which often doesn't make immediate sense to finite little us), lets him. So let's stop focusing on what Satan is doing to us and ask instead, "Why, God, are *you* allowing thus-and-so to happen to us? Is there a purpose?" (Sometimes there may not be one other than that Satan and the world are continuing to pour out their hatred against Jesus Christ by attacking the members of his body. But it never hurts to ask!) Frankly, I believe that if we concentrate on wrestling with God, any problems we have with the Devil will clear up.

If you're finding this concept of God controlling Satan hard to swallow, revisit some of the Scriptures we've looked at before. Consider that in the book of Job, Satan is, for all intents and purposes, irrelevant after the first two chapters. Job and his friends wrestle with what *God* is doing and why. And when the Lord finally comes to Job, it's not with a "the Devil made me do it" defense. God doesn't say, "You see, Job, old buddy, Satan was running you down, and I had this argument with him about how righteous you were. To try to prove he was right, he did all those nasty things to you." In fact, God never mentions Satan at all! And earlier in the book, though Satan is the one who has afflicted Job, God takes the responsibility for it (Job 2:3)! In 2 Corinthians 12:7–10, Paul talks about his thorn in the flesh as being a "messenger of Satan, to torment me," yet God's purpose behind it was not torment, but to keep Paul from becoming conceited about the heavenly revelations he had been witness to. God is the One who permitted Paul to have the thorn and who used Satan's evil intent for a good result. And when Paul wanted the thorn removed, he didn't rebuke Satan, or attempt to cast out the "demon of thorns," or even say, "In the power of Christ, I come against you, Devil!" No, he cried out to God! Why mess around with the underlings?

Consider the martyrs in Revelation 6. They ask the Lord how long it will be until he avenges their blood. Obviously, the persecutors who had murdered them would be held responsible. Yet the martyrs know that God can end the killings anytime he wants to. And the answer they are given is that they need to "wait awhile longer, until the number of their fellow servants and brothers *who were to be killed as they had been* was completed" (emphasis mine). God had a plan that involved allowing an exact number of Christians to be killed, and when that number was reached, he would pour out his wrath upon the killers. God, not the killers, is the One who is in control. (As an aside, the book of Revelation views those who have been martyred as receiving a special honor, so God's plan is not as cold and cruel as it might sound. In fact, this might be a partial answer as to why God allows us to suffer. Suffering for Christ in his eyes is a blessing, an honor, and it links us to Jesus, the Suffering Servant himself. Human eyes, though, see it as something to be avoided.)

> Since God is in control, we need to keep focused on him and keep dealing with him as we wrestle to try to get answers, or changes, or the strength to persevere.

Since God is in control, we need to keep focused on him and keep dealing with him as we wrestle to try to get answers, or changes, or the strength to persevere. We can keep focused on him by referencing him in our daily conversations, and certainly in our thoughts. We need to say aloud to others, and silently to ourselves, such things as these: "I'm not sure what God is up to in my life right now, but I'm asking him"; "When God decides I've had enough, he will deliver me"; "The Lord gives and the Lord takes away; may the name of the Lord be praised"; "Satan may be out to get me, but too bad for him that I'm the Lord's"; "Living in this fallen world, with its aches, pains, and heartaches, is wearing me down, but through Christ's power I can persevere and overcome the world"; "The demonic realm intends for all this to destroy me, but God will use all of it for my good and his honor."

I was shocked when I first met a young woman who would admit, "God's making me really angry today," particularly when I could see other reasons than divine intervention for the problems she was having. But I have come to see that she was right. Though she believed in free will and I was supposed to be the Calvinist who held to predestination, her practical, day-to-day understanding of God's sovereignty and complete control was stronger than mine. She knew how to stare God in the face, and her boldness allowed her to continue believing in him through good times and bad. I hope you, my reader, learn to do this, too.

As an added benefit of learning this "staring God in the face" move well, you will find your worship experiences enhanced because you will be worshiping the untamed, exciting, mysterious, sovereign, supremely powerful, unpredictable Creator and Sustainer of the universe, instead of, perhaps unconsciously and unwittingly, worshiping a little deity who is just like us, trying to do his best and hold his own against forces threatening to overwhelm him, but finding it all just a bit too much. Or praising the "gentle" Jesus who wishes he could help us (but can't) and that we'd, for once, love one another just the way we are and eat our vegetables (but, of course, he can't really make us).

Fasting is another technique that spiritual wrestlers occasionally use to keep focused in on God, staring him in the face. To fast is to go without food for a period of time. (Consult your doctor and possibly a spiritual mentor before attempting this spiritual discipline.) Fasting allows you to zero in on God, because every time your stomach rumbles or you feel a pang, you'll remember that you are hungry and you'll remember *why* you are hungry and shoot off another prayer to the Lord. And most fasters will use the time that would normally be utilized for preparing, eating, and cleaning up after a meal for prayer, Bible reading, and meditation. Some biblical references for fasting are Acts 13:1–3 (God reveals to the early church which of its teachers to send out as missionaries); Esther 4 (Mordecai, Esther, and the Jews were wrestling with God over their fates); Joel 2:12–18 (The entire nation gets serious when it comes to repenting). Fasting can help you hold fast to the Lord. (Ouch! That one was bad, I know!)

The Primary Hold: Wrapping Your Arms around the Past

Sometimes, you might mistakenly think that God has slipped out of your grasp and is heading for the arena's exit, but actually he's just shifted his weight, or his garment brushed against your arm, giving you the impression that he was leaving, but he's still standing right there with you. Also, God, like the old radio show super hero, "The Shadow," has the power to cloud humans' minds. He can make himself invisible to you so that he is "hiding" right in front of you. How, then, can you discern where your opponent is in relation to you?

Let's face it, there will probably be times in your life when all you can see are problems stacked on top of problems all around you, and God is nowhere in sight. You look in vain, not only for his personal presence, but also even just for signs that God wants to have a relationship with you and to bless you. In these kinds of circumstances, you need to look back at Jesus Christ and the cross. What better proof could be offered that God wants to be with us than that he came to earth as a man who was called "Immanuel, God with us" (Matthew 1:23)? What greater proof that God loves you could there be than that the Father sacrificed the Son so that you could be redeemed and spend eternity with him?

As I write these words, our congregation is ministering to a student who is dying of leukemia. Even pastors get tongue-tied in cases like this. What can you say? All the chemo that was tried these past two years ultimately failed. The young man has spent the better part of his nineteenth year in a hospital room. The family members have had to watch their

> People in the Bible often called to their minds what God had done for them in the past. They knew that it was the basis of God's relationship with them in the present.

beloved son, brother, and friend go steadily downhill. How can they be sure that God loves them and is still with them? Not by looking at their circumstances, that's for sure! I've counseled them to look back at the Christ who suffered for them. And I'm trying to do the same through my tears and heartache.

When the present is too confusing, and you can't see where God is or what he's doing now (and can you really trust your perception of things anyway?), turn instead to what he did in the past, his acts in history. The Psalms are full of the mighty deeds that God did for his people. Read them, and remind yourself that God is the same yesterday, today, and forever, so his character never changes.

The Old Testament people of God often called to their minds what God had done for them in the past. They knew that it was the basis of God's relationship with them in the present. For example, Exodus 12:1–28 established their practice of looking back to the night the Lord had freed them from four hundred years of slavery in Egypt. And Psalm 105 urged the people to look to the Lord for strength by remembering all he had done for their ancestors in the past.

Recalling God's activities in biblical times is helpful, but think, too, of your own personal past and how you have seen God at work. Remember answered prayer, guidance given, growth experienced, and how the Lord wooed you when he made you his own. If he did all that for you in the past, he certainly won't stop loving you now (Philippians 1:4–6)!

To clearly see that God is with you now, the past is where it's at! Let's listen to the apostle Paul:

> But God demonstrates his own love for us in this: While we were still sinners, Christ died for us. Since we have now been justified by his blood, how much more shall we be saved from God's wrath through him! For if, when we were God's enemies, we were reconciled to him through the death of his Son, how much more, having been reconciled, shall we be saved through his life! (Romans 5:8–10).

> What, then, shall we say in response to this? If God is for us, who can be against us? He who did not spare his own Son, but gave him up for us all—how will he not also, along with him, graciously give us all things? (Romans 8:31–32).

"Controlling" and "Pinning" God Down

Any idea of winning a match against God has to be tempered with an understanding of his graciousness and his desire to interact with us because, let's face it, you and I stand as much chance of pressuring God into submission as we do of winning a one-on-one basketball game with Kobe Bryant. If God wanted to, he could blow us away, or subdue us, by merely flexing his pinky or speaking a word. He is a whole lot bigger than you and I! Acknowledging this leads us to our next move.

Move #1: Using God's Strength against Him

Though using an opponent's strength against him may seem at first to be more related to Judo than to wrestling, wrestlers do it, too. A wrestler can step out of the way so that a lunging opponent goes flying into the turnbuckle. As an opponent is trying to force a wrestler down to the mat, the wrestler may suddenly fall to the

> You can use God's strength of character to pin him down.

mat voluntarily, so that the thrusting power of the antagonist will force him to fall as well. To beat God, we're likewise going to have to use his own strength because, comparatively speaking, you and I don't have any!

You can use God's strength of character to pin him down. Confront him using words such as these:

—"You are a God who loves justice, so vindicate me in the eyes of my friends and my enemies."

—"Jesus, your zeal for your Father's house consumed you, so take action to purify our church and end the divisive spirit found within it."

—"O God of boundless compassion, have mercy on me."

—"You are the All-Wise One, but I am not, so I need to come to you for answers."

—"You have the power to change things, so use that power."

—"Your name is holy, yet what I am going through is causing people to doubt you, so glorify your name."

You can use God's promises to pin him down. Here are some examples of the kinds of things to throw at him. "You've said if I seek you and your kingdom first, that you would meet my material needs. Well, I've been seeking, so start meeting!" "Jesus said that those who look for him will find him, so reveal yourself to me!" "You've promised to make me into the image of Christ, so grant me victory over this stubborn sin!" "Your word is not supposed to return to you void, but it sure seems like that is what's happening in my ministry. Do something about it!" "The promise is that the gates of hell wouldn't prevail against your church. Have you taken a look at our congregation lately?"

You can use God's revelations to give you some leverage. "Lord, you have shown that, though sometimes it takes a long time, you do come to the aid of your people. And even though I have been praying about my situation for a long time, I know that, even now, you can still take action." "Jesus had compassion on the crowd that seemed to be like sheep without a shepherd. Well, I feel pretty shepherdless. Have compassion on me and guide me." "Christ went around healing the sick, and so many Old Testament passages talk of physical salvation as well as spiritual salvation. I need some of that salvation now." "When the disciples came to you, Jesus, and asked you to explain what you were teaching in the parables to them, you did so. Please explain to me what you are trying to teach me in my life now."

Of course, in order to use God's strength of character, his promises, and his revelations to pin him down, you've got to *know* God's character, his promises, and his revelations. Yes, I'm talking about reading the Bible, studying the Bible, and mulling over, interacting with, and meditating on, what you find there. At this point, you may be saying, "Oh no! I paid good money for this book in order to learn the secrets of wrestling with God only to have the author tell me I've got to study the Bible more." I'm sorry, but you do. And I do. It's fundamental to the whole sport. You can't become a basketball player without learning how to dribble and pass. You can't be a golfer without learning the proper swing. You'll never go on the pro bowling circuit without learning how to hold your hand at the release so that the ball curves left, right, or goes straight down the lane. You will never get any good at spiritual wrestling if you don't know your Bible. Never. Period. End of discussion!

Or look at it this way. How can you possibly hope to prevail against your opponent if you never read any descriptions of his style or refuse to watch the "game films" of his matches?

One of the catechism teachers in my congregation shakes his head when he sees kids wearing "What would Jesus do?" bracelets. He says that they don't know what Jesus did when he was here bodily on earth the first time, so how could they possibly know what he would do today? And, unfortunately, he's right. They don't watch the game films, so they aren't familiar with his style. And one of the fascinating things about his style is that he seemed to tailor-fit it for each person and situation.

> The words "The Lord helps those who help themselves" aren't found in the Bible. But the concept definitely is there.

I don't mean to discourage you into thinking that you have to wait until you feel you thoroughly know the Bible before you can engage in any wrestling with God, or to imply that only Bible college teachers and seminary profs can do it. We can all wrestle with God using whatever we do know about the Scriptures. It's just that the more you know, the more effective you'll be as a spiritual wrestler and the more you'll get out of your personal experiences of grappling with God.

Move #2: Working at Solving Your Own Problems

Contrary to popular belief, the words "The Lord helps those who help themselves" aren't found in the Bible. But the concept definitely is there. The apostles urged their readers to work hard at growing in the faith because God had given them the means to do so. Peter wrote:

> His divine power has given us everything we need for life and godliness through our knowledge of him who called us by his own glory and goodness. Through these he has given us his very great and precious promises, so that through them you may participate in the divine nature and escape the corruption in the world caused by evil desires. For this very reason, make every effort to add to your faith goodness; and to goodness, knowledge; and to knowledge, self-control; and to self-control, perseverance; and to perseverance, godliness; and to godliness, brotherly kindness; and to brotherly kindness, love. For if you possess these qualities in increasing measure, they will keep you from being ineffective and unproductive in your knowledge of our Lord Jesus Christ.... Therefore, my brothers, be all the more eager to make your calling and election sure. For if you do these things, you will never fall, and you will receive a rich welcome into the eternal kingdom of our Lord and Savior Jesus Christ (2 Peter 1:3–8, 10–11).

Paul told the Christians in Philippi, "Continue to work out your salvation with fear and trembling, for it is God who works in you to will and to act according to his good purpose" (Philippians 2:12–13).

And, in the Old Testament, the book of Proverbs is full of practical advice about how people can get along in the world using human effort and not relying on unusual divine intervention. (Or maybe I should say that the advice depends on the normal, non-miraculous way that God permits the world and humans to work.) For examples, see Proverbs 6:6–11; 10:3–5; 11:25–26; 12:23, 25; 13:3; 19:19; 22:3, 6; 25:6–7.

To relate all of this to spiritual wrestling, sometimes we may have God pinned and not even realize it. We may be saying to God, "I need an answer about my future from you." And he responds, "Okay, I surrender. The answer is yours. I'll give it to you as you go seek advice from other believers, search the Scriptures, make a list of pros and cons regarding your upcoming decision, and sort through your desires." But because we're expecting something miraculous from his hand, and his technique in answering us seems so human and mundane, we miss the fact that he's already given us what we want. We may already know our answer using human logic, but we're waiting for God to speak. And all the while, God is saying, "I said I surrendered already. Hello? You can let me up now. Get off of my back!" We can remain deaf to him, though, if we fail to realize that he is often working through our efforts.

So while you wrestle with God, also pound the pavement looking for that new job, get a second and third medical opinion, look into alternate therapies, start packing for a move, go to a spiritual counselor, read books on the subject that's troubling you, or do whatever you can to work at solving the problem, or attaining the answer, or making the change that you seek. Remember that even Jacob made every human effort he could to placate Esau at the time he had his match with God. Jacob sent a generous gift of goats, ewes, rams, camels, cows, bulls and donkeys. (See Genesis 32:13–21.)

I wrestled with God over how my ministry could expand, but no supernatural insights came my way in dreams. My answers came in listening to my wife's advice when she urged me to put pen to paper, attend a seminar on becoming a Christian author, actually write articles and books, and sweat through rewrites. And God has now allowed me to reach a larger group of believers, but he used very human means to do so.

The Primary Hold: Clutching God's Masks and Working Them Off

Not only will God often concede a match and grant us our requests as we work to get our own answers or make our own changes, but he will often speak to us through unexpected, seemingly nonsupernatural means as well. If you think that God will only holler, "Uncle," while you're in church listening to a sermon, or in a voice that comes to you as you are having devotions, or through a revelation that your favorite TV preacher broadcasts via satellite, then you need to have your eyes opened to the many other ways God may choose to speak to you. Otherwise, God may be surrendering to you, and you won't realize it. He may be approaching you in one of his many "Masked Marvel" guises, while you are getting impatient waiting for your opponent to arrive.

The apostle Paul didn't believe that God only spoke through the Scriptures. In his letter to the Romans, he maintained that idolaters didn't have any excuse for worshiping their gods even if they hadn't received any specific prophetic revelation not to do so. Why? Because God had made it quite clear by the complexity and wonder of the world that only a Being such as he could have made it. Paul believed that God speaks to every human through creation and nature (Romans 1:18–23).

> Even unbelieving authors, thinkers, musicians, artists, and lawmakers may sometimes speak and promote God's truths when they are speaking from their hearts, even when they don't realize what they are doing.

Paul goes on to say that humans have God's law written on their hearts (Romans 2:14–15). So we might expect that even unbelieving authors, thinkers, musicians, artists, and lawmakers may sometimes speak and promote God's truths when they are speaking from their hearts, even when they don't realize what they are doing. Indeed, the Bible bears this out. When Paul witnessed to the Greeks in Athens, he quoted pagan poets (Acts 17:28–29). And, in what probably wasn't a favorite verse of the believers in ancient Crete, he quotes a Cretan prophet as saying, "Cretans are always liars, evil brutes, lazy gluttons" (Titus 1:12), and affirms that, "This testimony is true" (v. 13).

God's truth is everywhere! The theme song to the classic *Mary Tyler Moore Show* stated that "Love is all around," but the Bible asserts that God and his messages are all around. "The heavens declare the glory of God; the skies proclaim the work of his hands. Day after day they pour forth speech; night after night they display knowledge. There is no speech or language where their voice is not heard. Their voice goes out into all the earth, their words to the ends of the world" (Psalm 19:1–4a). "Holy, holy, holy is the LORD Almighty; the whole earth is full of his glory" (Isaiah 6:3).

Therefore, God may choose to take away someone's persistent fears by allowing that person to view a beautiful sunset over a lake and to realize that there is Someone much bigger who is in charge of everything. God once relieved my anxiety over a vote on denominational policy that my local governing board was taking by allowing me to see a herd of cattle on a hillside after I had stepped outside of the building where the meeting was taking place. The cattle were serenely munching away on the grass and seemed to say to me, "God's world will endure and go on no matter what the outcome of the vote is."

God has given me the encouragement I've needed to persevere in the ministry through lessons gleaned from, and examples given in, westerns, war movies, and adventure-oriented television series. The best of these have much to say about sacrificing for a cause, the necessity for individuals to "step up," and the effects of being in prolonged conflict.

Have you ever had a friend give you some advice, or even a mild rebuke, and realized later that it was exactly what God wanted you to hear? Any believer, not just the "professional Christians" like your pastor, has the potential to bring you a divine message. According to Peter, one of the hallmarks of these days when the Spirit is poured out on God's people is that anyone and everyone can prophesy (Acts 2:17–18)!

There are three keys to getting God's masks off so that you can realize when he is throwing in the towel and giving you what you desire or need. The first is that you simply must be aware that he sometimes speaks to us through what evangelical, Bible-believing Christians may call "unusual" or "unorthodox" means. If you are aware that such things may happen, you can be on the lookout for them. The second key, and I'm going to sound like a broken record here, is a thorough knowledge of the Bible, so you'll be able to recognize God's mannerisms and his messages when he comes to you in disguise. The third key is to have an expectant and thankful mind-set. If we concentrate only on our questions, struggles, concerns, needs, problems, and frustrations, they will become the only things we will be able to see. We won't notice that God is standing behind them, waiting for us to move them out of the way so that we can grapple with him and unmask him. Instead of focusing on negatives, we should always be hunting for God. Then we'll find him, even in out-of-the-way places. We'll start zeroing in on those "secular" or "natural" things in our world that reflect God—novels that sort of look like the Bible in some of their passages; our spouses who resemble Jesus today in their actions and attitudes toward us; that animal in

> Instead of focusing on negatives, we should always be hunting for God. Then we'll find him, even in out-of-the-way places.

the zoo that points to God's intelligent design in creation; meals provided for us when we're hungry that show God's care; and many, many other signs of God as well!

The best way to hunt for God is to obey Paul's commandments in Philippians 4:4–8:

> Rejoice in the Lord always. I will say it again: Rejoice! Let your gentleness be evident to all. The Lord is near. Do not be anxious about anything, but in everything, by prayer and petition, with thanksgiving, present your requests to God. And the peace of God, which transcends all understanding, will guard your hearts and your minds in Christ Jesus. Finally, brothers, whatever is true, whatever is noble, whatever is right, whatever is pure, whatever is lovely, whatever is admirable—if anything is excellent or praiseworthy—think about such things.

Hold #2: Constantly Pressing Down on God's Pressure Point

A pressure point is a place on the human body that, if strength is applied against it, will cause a person to crumble. God doesn't have a human body, but he has a pressure point just the same. His pressure point is his openness to hear prayer. The parables from Luke 11 and 18 that we looked at in our last chapter certainly teach that the way to get God to take some sort of action on our behalf is to keep asking him over and over again. Keep applying pressure to that point! And never, never, never give up!

This calls for faith on our parts. I don't know about you, but I hate to do things for no good reason. It's very hard for me to keep on praying about something when I don't see anything happening because of my efforts. However, in the old *Star Trek* series when Mr. Spock would place his hand on a Klingon's shoulder, it didn't seem as though much was being accomplished—until, that is, the Klingon slumped to the floor. Spock could work the pressure points. Likewise, the Bible calls on me to work God's pressure points. I need to believe what the Bible teaches—that my prayers are being heard, that they are "wearing God down," and that he's about to give in and answer. How do I know that my very next prayer won't be the one that presses on God's nerve just enough to cause him to surrender?

"Escaping" God's Seemingly Match-Ending Holds

Actually, escaping God isn't that hard to do, at least initially. You can rebel against his authority. You can know what he is telling you to do and stubbornly turn around and choose to do the opposite. You can decide to snub him, staying away from his people and his written Word, because he didn't answer a request the way you wanted him to. You can purposely decide to leave God out of your thinking and just live according to whatever seems right to you at any given moment. You can bad-mouth him to those around you. The problem is, though, that all these wrong choices merely prolong the inevitable, because if God is out to get you, he *will* get you, one way or another, one day or another. (He certainly got Paul—because God wanted him as an apostle to the Gentiles—didn't he! Even though Paul initially tried to wipe out Christianity—and Christians! See Acts 22:1–10; 26:12–18.)

No, what we are looking for is not so much an escape, as a reversal. In wrestling, a reversal occurs when an opponent has you, but you break, or slip away, and, as you do, you get your opponent in a hold of your own. Your opponent had seemingly been controlling you, but now you control him or her. Spiritual wrestlers look not to just escape God's control (which is impossible, anyway), but to reverse things and get God in their "control" (which he graciously sometimes allows to happen because it fits in with his plan for you).

The Primary Move: The Reversal

To execute a reversal you must argue with God after it seems he's already answered you and the match is over. Your arguments must be based, once again (you guessed it), on God's character, promises, and revelations.

A reversal of sorts happened in order to give me one of the "victories" I mentioned in chapter 5. Christian people were telling me that maybe I should be content to be single because my romantic relationships hadn't worked out, no one was on the horizon, and it seemed that this

> Your arguments must be based on God's character, promises, and revelations.

was God's will for me. However, I was able to answer them (and God?) back with the Scriptures and concepts I talked about in chapter 5. So I kept looking, kept dating, and God finally answered my prayers Yes.

Reversals have occurred when I have found myself questioning God about leaving unhealthy churches I was in. Biblical ideas that seemed to indicate that I should stay where I was would flood my mind. "Doctors aren't sent to well people, but to the sick." "Be content in all things." "Be willing to suffer for Christ." "The kingdom of God starts out small and then grows." But I would answer back, "The disciples shook the dust off of their feet and moved on when their ministry wasn't accepted. Pastors like me are supposed to *prepare* God's people for works of service, not *do* all the works of service! Jesus, you, yourself, couldn't stand a lukewarm congregation. It made you want to spit! And you threatened to close it, and another congregation that had lost its first love, down." I also used some human logic, much as Moses and the Gentile woman I mentioned in chapter 7 had done. I asked God, "Will it really benefit your kingdom to have me and the members of my family continue to deteriorate financially, physically, spiritually, and emotionally? With all of the churches in America, there must be one somewhere that would make better use of my gifts." And God did move us.

At this point, you may be asking me, "But how do you know whom you were really wrestling with? How do you know that it was God who brought those thoughts about staying into your mind? Maybe God wanted you to move all along, and Satan was just using Scripture to trip you up, much as he tried to do with Jesus in the wilderness?" The truth is, I don't know for sure whether the thoughts were from God or not, but practically speaking, it really doesn't make any difference whether they were from God, Satan, or my own mixed-up psyche, because the technique of grappling with who or whatever and getting a reversal is the same in any case—answering back with scriptural truths.

> How do you know whom you were really wrestling with? How do you know that it was God who brought those thoughts into your mind?

Answering back with scriptural truths and with human logic helped me win reversals. And they can help you win, too. But not every single time. God is still sovereign, after all. Lest you think I'm some sort of wrestling superstar, I'm not. I'm still learning about all of this, too. There have been plenty of times when God has pinned me and I tried to execute a reversal by saying, "I don't like this, and here are all the good reasons why things should change," but he replied, "My decision stands."

How we are to respond when God pins us and we lose a match, along with other issues involved with good sportsmanship as it applies to spiritual wrestling, will be explored in the next chapter.

It's Your Turn!

Here are some questions to stimulate your own thoughts as you interact with this chapter, either by yourself or in a group.

1. Think of a request you'd like to "convince" God to answer. What reasons, based on his character, promises, revelations, and on human logic, can you give him for doing so? It might be helpful to write them down. You may or may not want to share this with your group, if you are in one.

2. How real does God seem to you in your day-to-day living? Why?

3. What are the ways that God is showing love to you in your situation, whatever it is, right now?

4. Can you remember a time when you got a Christian insight from a nonbiblical or unchristian source? If you are in a group, can you share the insight and the source?

5. Since knowing and studying the Bible is of supreme importance for wrestling with God, how well would you say you know the Bible? How, practically speaking, do you think you could improve on that knowledge? What techniques, methods, programs, and guides have worked for you as you've attempted to study the Bible? Why? Which have left you cold? Why?

6. Which of the moves and holds of spiritual wrestling have you tried? Are you good at any of them? Which do you need to work on?

7. Are there any questions or concerns you have after reading this chapter?

Chapter 9

In spiritual wrestling, as in other competitions, there are good sports and bad sports. I'll list the rules pertaining to how to be a good sport and elaborate on them in this chapter.

Rule #1: No Cheating!

Professional wrestling's bad guys that you see on the cable television shows will sometimes cheat by bringing things into the ring that shouldn't be there. They will conceal brass knuckles, small hammers, nails, combs (for raking over people's eyes—ouch!), etc. But in spiritual wrestling, one cheats by *not* bringing into the ring something that *should* be there—namely, one's whole self.

The temptation in spiritual wrestling is to be less than honest with God. For example, if we're feeling angry with him, rather than admitting to it, we tend to give him the runaround by telling him we're "disappointed" in the way things have worked out, or that we're just "a little confused" right now, or that he needs to take all that we're saying with a grain of salt because we didn't get much sleep and are having a bad day. We're hesitant to bring our fears, doubts, struggles, and frustrations to him in total honesty.

So what God faces in the ring is less than who we really are at the moment. And our lack of honesty means that we could be charged with stalling or delaying the match because God will need to probe and get us to face up to what's really going on before the wrestling can begin in earnest. And he will do that. See how he dealt with Adam and Eve in Genesis 3:8–19, and how Jesus interacted with the Samaritan woman in John 4:7–26. We'll seem foolish if, while God is probing and questioning, we're standing there bemoaning, trying to hide what's really going on, or trying to change the subject, or working to find ways to answer him that will enable us to keep up our pretension that everything's really fine. Unfortunately, one sure way to lose a wrestling match is to just stand around doing nothing while your opponent is actively aggressive.

I admit that I have trouble being myself in the ring. My "proper" theology, or more accurately, my improper understanding and application of my "proper" theology have often led me to freeze up as my tongue gets tied up in knots. I'll pray something like, "Lord, I'm really mad about the way things are turning out, but, of course, how can I, with my limited knowledge, really judge how things are going, and what right do I, the pot, have to be upset with the potter anyway, so just forget I said anything, but, you know, I really am angry, and I feel that I must share that with you, but, of course, we're not supposed to let our emotions rule us, so help me conquer my anger, but conquering it would entail facing up to it, and I'm too ashamed in front of my Holy God to do that, so just skip it, Lord, except I'm still angry so … Oh, I give up!" Then I quit praying altogether and go check out the Popeye Message Boards on the Internet. However, running out of the ring is not exactly the way to win a fight.

Like me, people often think they have the best of motives for being less than honest with the Lord. He is their superior, after all, so they want to treat him with respect. Looking to the military can help us here, because there people can express displeasure with a superior's actions and decisions if they respectfully first request "Permission to speak freely, Sir," and that request is granted. God graciously grants us "permission to speak freely" and, as long as we remember that, we can be honest with him and respectful at the same time. We can also address our outpourings to God using equivalents of "Sir," such as "Lord," "My Master," "Heavenly Father," and "All-Knowing One."

The real problem with people like me is that we find it hard to be honest with the Lord because we are afraid that our anger, our frustration, and our confusion are sins. But biblical scholars are divided over whether or not it is really a sin to be angry or disappointed with God. The Bible certainly gives us examples of people who were honest about their reactions and feelings about what God was doing, and often God just deals with their concerns and answers their questions rather than rebuking

> The real problem with people like me is that we find it hard to be honest with the Lord because we are afraid that our anger, our frustration, and our confusion are sins.

them. Were they sinning? Maybe, but God didn't seem to treat them as if they were. Remember Abraham laughing at God? Yet, God didn't revoke his promise to him. And when his wife also laughed at God and then tried to cover up what she had done, the Lord wouldn't let her (Genesis 18:13–15). He made her face her emotions. Naomi told people that God had made her life bitter, yet God still worked to bless her. Jeremiah expressed his extreme displeasure (and that's putting it mildly) at what he had to suffer as a prophet of the Lord, even claiming that God had deceived him, yet the Lord's prophet he remained. The Lord also allowed the words of the author of Ecclesiastes to have a place in the Holy

Bible, although they express a bleak outlook on life and counter-balance more positive statements and concepts found in Psalms and Proverbs. And Jesus wasn't afraid to cry out and ask his Father why he had forsaken him.

And even if, in some cases, it is a sin to harbor strong emotions and opinions about the Lord in your heart and mind, it's still beneficial to admit what's going on inside. Then God can convict you if convict you he will, and you can repent of it all so you can be forgiven. God doesn't want us to cover up sin (Psalm 32:1–5; Proverbs 28:13; 1 John 1:8–2:2)!

Consider that perhaps your being angry with God is actually a sign of your faith in God. You aren't blaming fate or just feeling down on your luck. Instead, you hold Someone responsible for what's happened to you or what you're going through. You believe that there is a God there to be mad at.

And let's remember what kind of God he is. God is the All-Knowing One. If we attempt to cover up what's going on inside of us, we are implicitly saying (whether wittingly or unwittingly) that

> Consider that perhaps your being angry with God is actually a sign of your faith in God.

we believe God to be less than he really is, that somehow we think that this time we're going to get away with fooling him. It's actually blasphemous, when you come right down to it. Rather than presenting a god who can be deceived, the Bible presents the God who knows exactly what's going on (1 Samuel 15; Proverbs 20:27; Jeremiah 3:10; John 2:23–25). And we should treat him as such.

Rule #2: Don't Be an Insufferable Winner!

I've known people who have had powerful encounters with God and who have then assumed that they should immediately be placed in positions of spiritual leadership in their local churches. Depending on the person, that can be an "accident waiting to happen."

In my younger days, I moved in charismatic circles more than I do now. I remember one student who received a prophetic inter-pretation of a tongue that seemed to be legitimate. However, after-ward he got a swelled head and became a self-appointed "prophet" for the group, even though his "revelations" were no longer being confirmed by other, more mature and gifted members.

His pronouncements were taken less and less seriously and, regrettably, the members of the fellowship group started to ignore him. Frankly, he made us feel uncomfortable every time he had a "new" word of prophecy. Eventually, he quit coming out to the Bible studies and prayer meetings and stopped moving about in Christian circles altogether. Many years later, I had a bittersweet reunion with him during one of our town's annual festivals. In the course of our conversation, it became evident that, while he was happy to learn I was still into that Christian thing, he no longer was. And he liked it that way. As I walked away from him, I was saddened to know that pride had destroyed a young Christian's relationship with the Lord.

Later on, in one church I pastored, a woman who had been on a "great" mission trip came back and proceeded to imply that the rest of us in the congregation were unspiritual and deceived. If only we could have participated in the devotions at the work camp! Then we'd know what "true joy" in the Lord was. You might imagine how this made me, as her pastor, feel. I had to sit there while she waxed poetic about what a godly leader the man who had led devotions and Bible studies was, and how he always hit the nail right on the head with his messages, and how she came to life under his teach-ing in a way that she never had before. It seemed that, according to what she was saying, I might just as well have resigned right then and there to make room for the congregation to be ministered to by a *real* leader. Ironically, I happened at the time to be counseling that same man who was her spiritual idol. He was struggling with a spiritual life he felt was going nowhere fast and was even doubting his own salvation. But, of course, professional ethics forbade me to tell the woman about any of that! Right around this same time, she and one of her friends finally began to lose weight "with the Lord's help." "The Lord" not only told them what to eat each day, but also how many sit-ups they should do. Then, "the Lord" began telling them other things, too—such as what was wrong with our church, our lay leadership, and me as the pastor. When they failed to convince the elders and the deacons that theirs were the true words of God, they and their families left the church, causing much confusion, heartache, and frustration among church members who couldn't understand what had happened to "those nice people," and among the church leaders who felt they couldn't even speak the same language as the women, much less reach out to them anymore. And I gained a new ulcer or two in the process!

In both the cases of the woman and the student who appointed themselves as prophets, spiritual breakthroughs were misinterpreted as signs that the recipients must be *very special people,* at least in their own eyes, and should be *respected as such* by everyone who belonged to the Lord. Years of pastoral experience has taught me that in most cases the person has a serious issue with feeling insecure and often will use "spirituality" to bolster their self-esteem.

> If you win one or more matches with God, don't take giant steps backward in your relationship with him by becoming full of pride.

If you win one or more matches with God and receive wisdom-filled insights, or a spectacular answer to prayer, or a new closeness with the Lord, or a rock-solid faith, or whatever, don't take giant steps backward in your relationship with him by becoming full of pride—something that the Lord abhors (Proverbs 6:16–19; 8:12–13; 21:4)! Proverbs 16:18 even uses a wrestling term when it says, "Pride goes before destruction, a haughty spirit before a *fall*" (emphasis mine). And don't expect that others should instantly acknowledge what a "spiritual giant" you are and want to have you as one of their leaders. In fact, the Bible warns against a church hastily choosing its leaders. Potential leaders must be those who have been tried and have proven true (1 Timothy 3:1–10; 5:22).

Winning a match with God doesn't make one a "spiritual giant" anyway. Does anyone doubt that the Lord could have done a lot more to Jacob than just wrenching his hip during their bout? It was by the grace of God that Jacob "prevailed." And if you have "prevailed," it was only by that same grace. Remember what was said in chapter 8 about "pinning" God by using his strength against him, and about getting answers by realizing that, as you work, God is working within you, and about taking advantage of God's openness to hearing prayers, and about executing reversals by relying on what God has revealed in his Word. Notice that we couldn't accomplish any of these things without God and what he has done. In a very real sense, we don't beat God; he beats himself!

Rule #3: Don't Be a Sore Loser!

When God wins and pins you to the mat by saying No to a prayer request, or by letting you know that there are some things you can't, or aren't ready to, understand, or by showing you that your situation won't improve until you change some things about yourself, or by convicting you of sin, or by proving that your assumptions were wrong, or by however he does it, be gracious when he lets you up. Don't storm out of the gym declaring that this is the last time you'll ever have anything to do with the Lord.

Follow the examples of the All-Stars. They knew how to accept defeat. When Nathan pointed out David's sin, the king confessed it (2 Samuel 12:13) and then pleaded with God, fasting and lying on the ground during the night, for the life of the son that the Lord had said would die. But after David heard that the child had died, verses 20–23 tell us:

> Then David got up from the ground. After he had washed, put on lotions and changed his clothes, he went into the house of the LORD and worshiped. Then he went to his own house, and at his request they served him food, and he ate.
>
> His servants asked him, "Why are you acting this way? While the child was alive, you fasted and wept, but now that the child is dead, you get up and eat!"
>
> He answered, "While the child was still alive, I fasted and wept. I thought, 'Who knows? The LORD may be gracious to me and let the child live.' But now that he is dead, why should I fast? Can I bring him back again? I will go to him, but he will not return to me."

David was willing to let a match be over when it was over, instead of constantly revisiting it, as we are often prone to do, which in the end only wears us down.

And Job, though he didn't receive the kind of answer from God that he was expecting, accepted and even embraced the answer the Lord did give, humbling himself in the face of God's greatness. "My ears had heard of you but now my eyes have seen you. Therefore I despise myself and repent in dust and ashes" (Job 42:5–6).

Paul was literally floored by God and told the way things were going to be on the road to Damascus. He responded with obedience (Acts 26:19). And, later, though his "thorn" wasn't removed, he accepted that God still loved him and that God's grace would continue to operate in his life, thorn or no.

Like the All-Stars, we, too, will be called upon to accept God's victories. It will help us do so if we remember that the One who triumphs over us is our loving heavenly Father, not a bully, or one who is going to brag about what he did to us, or a sadist who takes delight in hurting us, or an egotist who needs to crush others so he can feel important. No, he is the One who is working all things for our ultimate good (Romans 8:28).

Hebrews 12:1–13 makes the point that even continued persecution, as it is used by God to discipline his people, can be beneficial. The author quotes Proverbs 3:11–12 and reminds the readers that the Lord disciplines those he *loves* (emphasis mine). He says that our earthly fathers' discipline led to our respecting them. He exclaims, "How much more should we submit to the Father of our spirits and live!" (Hebrews 12:9). Our earthly fathers disciplined us "as they

> David was willing to let a match be over when it was over, instead of constantly revisiting it, which in the end only wears one down.

thought best," but he goes on to say that "God disciplines us for our good, that we may share in his holiness" (v. 10). Discipline is unpleasant but, "Later on, however, it produces a harvest of righteousness and peace for those who have been trained by it" (v. 11). Therefore, the author urges us to be strong under discipline (vv. 12–13). This applies to spiritual wrestling in that, sometimes, God's victories over us will entail discipline.

But even when they don't, the principles in Hebrews 12 can still apply to our bouts with God. Just as discipline is beneficial to us, even when we lose a match with God, we end up winning! God will use our loss in our best interests. He can teach us or train us through it. And he, like any good parent, can use the word "No" to spare his child complications, trouble, temptations, and injury. Therefore, let's be strong even in the midst of defeat! Let's humbly submit ourselves to God and accept what he says, does, and instructs us to do. Let's not rebel, or turn away from him, or snub him, or bad-mouth him. Instead let's say, "The better person won, Lord," and remember that we can be better people ourselves because of it.

And, while being angry with God may or may not be a sin (as we saw earlier), certainly *remaining angry* with God over a long period of time is. It means that one is refusing to trust that God knows what he's doing, or that he really loves us, or that he has our best interests at heart. If we stay angry, we aren't submitting to our sovereign God, our King. If you find yourself still angry at God over the outcome of a match long since over, you will need to confess this to him and work hard at consciously and continually letting go of the anger and accepting God as God. You may have to wrestle with yourself! There have been times when I have had to violently shake my head as a way to clear my mind and forcefully remind myself that I'm not going to let my thoughts go down certain avenues. If this sounds kind of weird to you, consider that Paul told the Christians "I beat my body and make it my slave so that after I have preached to others, I myself will not be disqualified for the prize" (1 Corinthians 9:27). I'm not saying that if you have persistent, angry thoughts against God you need to physically beat yourself, but use whatever works for you. Better to deal strongly with wrong thinking than to have God or his people break off any encounters with you because they know you're a sore loser.

Rule #4: Be Gracious over the Long Haul

In chapter 5, I said that sometimes a match with God seems to end in a tie, with no clear-cut victor. And so we have to climb back in the ring with him again, and possibly again, and possibly yet again before anything is really decided or resolved. In fact, sometimes our wrestling with God takes the form of an ongoing rivalry. When that happens, we need to, first of all, make sure we don't grow weary of facing off with the Lord. I remember some of the greatest all-time sports rivalries of the past like the Los Angeles Lakers versus the Boston Celtics and Chris Evert versus Martina Navratilova. The Lakers didn't sigh when they had to face Boston in the play-offs, and Chris didn't say, "Oh no, not Martina again!" (At least, not to my knowledge, they didn't.) They usually came across in the press as being eager to face their rivals because they knew it would be

> Let us not become weary in tussling with God, for at the proper time we will reap a harvest if we don't give up.

exciting and would bring out the best in everybody involved. The opponents, "trash talking" aside, usually spoke respectfully of each other, appreciating the strengths and talents that the other had. In an ongoing rivalry with God, be eager to climb back into the ring with him again, knowing that eventually it will bring out the best in you and will give you a deeper appreciation of his character, abilities, and attributes. And speak respectfully of your rival to others.

Galatians 6:9 exhorts its readers to keep on doing good to others, saying, "Let us not become weary in doing good, for at the proper time we will reap a harvest if we do not give up." Though this verse doesn't talk about spiritual wrestling, the principle found here applies to our bouts with God. Let us not become weary in tussling with God, for at the proper time we will reap a harvest if we don't give up.

However often your heart says, "Seek his face," may your answer be, "Your face, LORD, I will seek" (Psalm 27:8).

Rule #5: Respect and Encourage Your Fellow Wrestlers

As you wrestle with God, you'll meet others who are engaged in their own bouts with God, too. Chances are, you'll feel a spirit of kinship and camaraderie with them. You'll want to share "war stories," things you've learned, etc. Just remember as you do so to respect the experiences that the others are having with God, and how God is dealing with them during their matches. Resist any temptation to jump in and end their matches quickly by telling them definitively what the Lord is trying to teach them through what's happening, or what the Lord's answers to their queries are. While it is true that the Lord can use you as his instrument to end someone else's match, be careful not to make the same mistake that Job's friends did and easily and readily presume to know all there is to know about the unfathomable mind of God. Instead, we can preface our ruminations that we share with our fellow wrestlers by saying, "*Maybe* the Lord is doing thus-and-so because . . . ," or "Could it be that . . . ," or "Have you ever considered . . . ," or "Perhaps this part of the Bible applies . . ." Besides, telling someone, "Your match could be over if you'd just do thus-and-so," belittles the struggling that he or she has gone, or is going, through, and could be interpreted as implying that the wrestler was stupid or spiritually blind for not seeing the "obvious solution."

Our goals should be to encourage one another in our matches, to exhort one another to hang in there, to remind one another of the benefits and necessities of grappling with God, to talk about the love behind God's moves, and to call to mind that it is God's own strength that enables us to confront him. See 1 Samuel 23:16; Proverbs 27:17; Acts 14:21–22; 15:32; Romans 1:11–12; Hebrews 10:25.

As a Christian, I have been helped the most by people who shared those goals, as opposed to well-meaning folks who tried to give me quick, authoritative "answers" to whatever questions or circumstances were troubling me. How could those folks know any answers anyway, if they hadn't wrestled with God awhile over my concerns? As a pastor, I have been the most helpful when I kept those goals in mind, instead of trying to be "Mr. Answer Man." How could I have known the answers to other people's concerns if I haven't wrestled with God for a while over them?

We'll explore more about our interaction with other wrestlers in chapter 10.

It's Your Turn!

Here are some questions to stimulate your thoughts as you interact with this chapter, either by yourself or in a group.

1. Has there ever been a time when the Lord cut through all your pretenses and got to the heart of the matter between him and you, even though you were trying to hide things from him?

2. In this chapter, it was said that when we try to cover up, instead of being honest before God, we are implying that God is less than he is, that he isn't the All-Knowing One. Are there other things we think, say, or do that send the message (even unintentionally) that God is less than he claims to be?

3. Do you think it's a sin to be angry with God? Why or why not?

4. What can you do to avoid being caught up in spiritual pride?

5. Are you involved, or have you been involved, in any long-term bouts with God? If so, what do, or did, they concern? How are they going, or how did they go? How have they affected your view of, and attitude toward, God?

6. How, practically speaking, can you encourage others? What sort of encouragement do you need the most from others?

7. Are there any questions or concerns you have after reading this chapter?

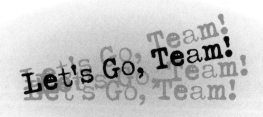

Chapter 10

Let's Go, Team!

While wrestling with God can be an intensely personal experience, none of us were meant to keep encountering God, or to build a relationship with him, totally on our own.

The Old Testament is the story of God establishing the Jews as the "people of God." It's not the story of God just choosing willy-nilly to bless certain individuals. And the New Testament makes it clear that when one becomes a Christian, one also becomes a member of the church of Jesus Christ, the *new* "people of God." For example, Ephesians 2:19–22 and 1 Peter 2:9–10 paint pictures of the church as the new Israel. They do this by applying to Christians some Old Testament phrases that were originally used to describe the Jews as God's chosen people. To become a Christian, then, is to become a member of a large group of people who believe in, and are called by, God. This means that you will need to interact with others and they with you. (Romans 12:1–16; 1 Corinthians 12; and Ephesians 4:1–16 give us some of God's guidelines for doing so.)

To put all of this in wrestling terms, when you wrestle with God, you are not just competing as an individual; you are part of a team. You have responsibilities toward others, and they have responsibilities toward you. We'll examine some of these in this chapter.

I'm Flagging, So I'm Tagging

Some physical wrestling bouts that you see on TV are "tag-team" matches. Let's say that good old Muscles McGerk is a member of a tag team. This means that if Muscles is grappling with an opponent in the ring but finds that he can't get the upper hand, or starts to get tired, or has weakened his rival but just can't seem to put him down, then Muscles can go over to the ropes and tag his partner who is outside of the ring. The partner will switch places with Muscles and resume the fight. And when the partner needs a break, he will tag Muscles. And on it goes.

Often when I'm wrestling with God, particularly if the match is a prolonged one, I feel that I am nearing the end of my resources. So I will "tag" a Christian author by snatching his or her book off my shelf. I might involve a wise Christian friend in my fight by using the phone, email, or by arranging a lunch meeting. I can benefit from insights and spiritual energy that are not my own and use these as I renew my tussle with the Lord. I remember one time when I couldn't wind down and catch a precious spiritual breath and get some needed rest because I was still revved up from wrestling with God about my future. My roommate placed his hands on my head and prayed simply, "Lord, let Steve get some sleep." Suddenly, I began to feel a warm and relaxing sensation traveling down my body. I say "began to feel" because I was asleep before it worked its way down. And when I was wrestling with God over my marital status, or more precisely my lack thereof, my mother and grandmother prayed for me. Mom even threw some cold "spiritual water" in my face to try to bring me to my senses when I was complaining to her that, as a pastor in a small church, it was almost impossible to meet single women. She said, "Who knows? God could have your future wife walk through the doors of your church and join your congregation." And she was right. God did. Mom and Grandma prayed regularly for my ministry, and I know that, over the years, any spiritual victories I won or helped others win didn't come about because I'm a strong intercessor, but because I had partners who were.

Like me, when you are spiritually wrestling, you'll find that it's good to "tag" other people and get them involved in praying for you and with you about your concerns. It helps to get others searching the Scriptures with you to find answers or to discover more of God's strengths that can be used against him. And when you get weary and need to catch your breath and

> When you are spiritually wrestling, you'll find that it's good to "tag" other people and get them involved in praying for you and with you about your concerns.

regain some energy, it's nice to have someone else there to encourage you and help you find the strength to go on.

Of course, in order for others to get involved in your fight, they need to know that you are fighting. They need to know your prayer requests, your questions, your doubts, and your struggles. So you must be honest with them. To refuse to admit that you're wrestling with God is to deprive yourself of the help that could be available, or the answers that God may give through other Christians.

I can remember two men, who, in moments of uncharacteristic openness, told me that they were having problems with their wives and had even contemplated divorce. But when, as their pastor, I tried to follow up and arrange for some counseling, they held me off at arm's length. And later, when I would ask how things were going at home, they would quickly answer, "Fine! Just fine!" and change the subject. Anybody observing them and their families could see that things were far from being "just fine," but there wasn't much I could do to help the men, since they wouldn't admit it to themselves. It was obvious to everyone else that God was whacking them over the head with spiritual two-by-fours and twisting their arms, imploring them to engage him, while they tried to ignore the fact that they were in the ring with him and instead pretended they were at home, sitting in their recliners, watching movies.

Don't be like them. Be open with others about the bouts you're having with the Lord. Being open entails some risk, to be sure. But, so what? If you're willing to climb into the ring with God, then you're no stranger to risk-taking! There's a risk that the person you open up to may call you a heretic because you have doubts or questions, or that the person you talk to may form a lower opinion of you because the realization dawns on them that you're not perfect, or that the person you confide in may broadcast your intimate secrets to others. If the person you turn to does any of those things, it shows that he or she hasn't yet understood what the normal Christian life is all about.

> Wrestling with God is *the normal Christian* life. So why should you be afraid to admit that you do it?

If you take nothing else away from this book, I hope you recognize that wrestling with God is *the normal Christian* life. So why should you be afraid to admit that you do it? Those who look at spiritual wrestlers as though they are from Mars probably haven't yet been trained in the sport and don't understand what it's all about. They are like me as I described myself in chapter 1 before I became a hockey fan—totally confused as to what all the struggles, sweat, sound, and fury is all about. They are showing themselves to be too immature or inexperienced to be part of a tag team. If you have encountered these types of people and have been hurt by them (I know I have!), it doesn't mean that you should stop looking for, and reaching out toward, other potential teammates. Good wrestlers are out there! If I was choosing a tag-team partner for physical wrestling and naively picked Alan Alda and subsequently got my team's clock cleaned in the ring, should I then walk past Mr. T and Hulk Hogan in the lobby as they wait around to be enlisted on a team? It's not as though you need to open up to everybody or just anybody about your wrestling with God. You can choose people you can trust to be your tag team-mates, people who have some level of spiritual maturity and experience in the ring with God. The right somebodies won't look down on you. They will understand. And when you find a spiritual Mr. T, it will more than compensate for the bouts you lost alongside a Mr. Alda.

Who knows? Maybe you can be a Mr. T for someone else! Be on the lookout for other wrestlers who may be in need of a partner to tag. Make it your goal to be the kind of person others feel they can be honest around. An accepting, helpful, nonjudgmental, "we're all in this together" spirit is required, as well as a willingness to listen for twice as long as you talk. As I said in the last chapter, when you offer advice or insight, do so gently. And, whatever you do, don't name your team "Job's Comforters!"

Fans in the Stands

If you were a member of a high-school or college wrestling team and your team was at a tournament, what would be expected of you while your teammates were engaging in their bouts? Would it be okay if you started talking to the other spectators around you about politics or a new television program that you enjoy? Should you hang around the refreshment area most of the day? How about if you flirted the afternoon away with members of the opposite sex in the parking lot?

If you were on a team, you would be expected to be in the gymnasium or arena, paying attention to what was going on and cheering for your teammates. You would be expected to act like a fan. Your presence, your attention, and your cheers would encourage your teammates. And they, in turn, would be expected to do the same for you when it's your turn to step out onto the mat.

Well, on Sunday mornings and at other times when Christians are assembling together for worship, fellowship, service projects, or Bible studies, there will be those among your teammates there who will be wrestling with God. They will need to be encouraged, and your presence and participation will help do that. Having gone through bouts of my own with the Lord, I know what it does for my spirits to look around in church at my teammates on a Sunday morning and be reminded that I am not the only one who believes in God and is attempting to fight the good fight. Often, because we Christians are out in the world during the week and are constantly confronted by its values even when we're at home (thanks to the mass media), we can start to feel like Elijah, who said to the Lord at one point, "I am the only one left" (1 Kings 19:14). But God immediately mentioned the names of others who served him and told Elijah, "Yet I reserve seven thousand in Israel—all whose knees have not bowed down to Baal and all whose mouths have not kissed him" (1 Kings 19:18). God uses Christian gatherings to remind us that he has reserved many others who don't serve the idols of this world.

Hebrews 10:23–25 (a passage I've referenced before) says:

> Let us hold unswervingly to the hope we profess, for
> he who promised is faithful. And let us consider how we
> may spur one another on toward love and good deeds.
> Let us not give up meeting together, as some are in the
> habit of doing, but let us encourage one another—and all
> the more as you see the Day approaching.

Notice that holding unswervingly to our hope, spurring one
another on, and encouraging one another are mentioned alongside of the command to not give up meeting together. It's been my
experience, and that of countless others, that these things are
closely linked.

So here is another reason to keep attending worship services,
Bible studies, and small group meetings even if you don't feel like it,
or are currently having a hard
time in your relationship with the
Lord, or have been disappointed
and depressed by the way that
one of your bouts ended. We
keep attending because we're not
just doing it for ourselves. Our
attendance is a ministry to others.
We can encourage our team-

> I know what it does for
> my spirits to look around at
> my teammates on a Sunday
> morning and be reminded
> that I am not the only one
> attempting to fight the good
> fight.

mates just by showing up and participating! We can encourage them
by singing alongside of them. We can encourage them by paying
attention when they offer a prayer, or a special musical number, or a
testimony, or an announcement about an opportunity for service.
There's nothing that will make a person feel like bailing out of
matches with God, if not the Christian life altogether, more than

preparing something to exhort the team or lift its morale and then having the team not show up!

Some churches I have pastored were conducting regular, weekly Sunday evening services that, to be honest, had seen their better days, attendance wise. We who still came out to them knew in our hearts that it was true that where two or three gathered together the Lord was present, but it still bothered us that the majority of his people stayed away. We would have to fight bad thoughts toward the rest of the congregation all during the service. Weren't the Word of God and fellowship important to them? We would leave the services feeling very much like Elijah—very lonely. And the worship at the services was less than dynamic. I remember one poorly attended song service when the song leader sincerely asked the spiritual equivalent of the old line that stand-up comedians who were bombing used, "What is this, an audience or an oil painting?" He said, "Is anybody singing out there? The only one I can hear is Pastor Steve!" (It's not that I'm a great singer, but I do have a loud voice.)

As a pastor, I'm far from being immune to the frustrations of poor attendance. If you want to do something for your pastor, show up! Many pastors feel as though they have been called by God to coach a team, except that the team never bothers to come to the practices and team meetings!

And speaking of pastors and coaches brings us to our next point.

Respect for the Coaches

A couple of years ago, I saw Magic Johnson being interviewed on TV by a team of sportscasters. Magic called two of the broadcasters by their first names, but the third he always referred to as "Coach," and, indeed, the man was a former basketball coach. I realized that Magic, throughout his high-school, college, and pro-fessional basketball careers, had been taught to respect and respond to his coaches. He had personally seen the value of coach-ing, so that even though he was not under the broadcaster's author-ity in any way, he still couldn't bring himself to address the man by a title other than the respectful "Coach." As I write these words, Shaquille O'Neal and the Los Angeles Lakers have just won their third consecutive NBA championship. When asked by a reporter what part coach Phil Jackson played in the team's triumph, Shaquille said that, without Phil Jackson, he had no championship rings, but with Phil, he has three. Star athletes, like Magic and Shaq, recognize the importance of their coaches.

As a spiritual wrestler, you will find that many coaches have been divinely assigned to teach you, train you, and help you realize your dream of growing in your relationship with the Lord. A coach is someone who knows the sport, is experienced in it, and is able to pass on what he or she has learned to others. Spiritual wrestling coaches can be pastors, Sunday-school teachers, youth group leaders, camp counselors, professors, parents, grandpar-ents, friends, conference speak-

> When you realize who your coaches are, listen to them and respect them, even if they aren't flashy or exciting or perfect or pretty.

ers, authors, members of your small group, older church members—anyone who fits the definition given above. When you realize who your coaches are, listen to them and respect them, even if they aren't the most flashy or exciting people around, or have some idiosyncrasies, or aren't up on contemporary music or pop culture, or aren't perfect, or aren't pretty, or aren't (at least at first glance) the types of personalities that would have been first on your list of potential mentors.

At my college, I was privileged to study under two legendary Bible professors whose wisdom, intelligence, vibrancy, unique personalities, and, yes, antics, had kept students enthralled for years and years. There was another prof who was quieter and unassuming. His name wasn't instantly associated with the school as the other profs' names were. He didn't get all the accolades or have stories told about him, but he was one of the first people who really opened up the Old Testament to me.

Because I attended a Christian college, I had opportunities to hear many famous musical groups and soloists. After all these years, there are still some concerts I can remember and some that are lost to the passage of time. One concert I do recall that ministered to my soul in ways some others didn't was simply a friend of mine, his sister, and her boyfriend in a small-town church sincerely singing about, and testifying for, Jesus. Their concert reminded me that you don't have to be rich or famous to be used by the Lord, that he even chooses people like me, and that the spirit behind a worship time is just as important as the content.

Coaches aren't always the attention getters. But they are the ones who minister to you, teach you, and help you in your matches with God.

And we can minister to our coaches, as well. Turning back to Hebrews again, in chapter 13, verse 7, there's an admonition regarding our spiritual wrestling coaches: "Remember your leaders, who spoke the word of God to you. Consider the outcome of their way of life and imitate their faith." Later in the same chapter, the author says, "Obey your leaders and submit to their authority. They keep watch over you as men who must give an account. Obey them so that their work will be a joy, not a burden, for that would be of no advantage to you" (v. 17). Our actions and attitudes toward our coaches, and whether or not they can see that we are attempting to do what they are teaching us, will have an effect on them. We will have a part in determining whether they view their coaching work as a joy, or as a burden. And as we minister to them, we're actually benefiting ourselves, because if their work becomes a burden, we won't get anything out of it. If you've ever been in a group that was led by a leader who acts as though he or she is just marking time, you know what the writer of Hebrews is getting at.

Spiritual coaches, if you are reading this book, notice that Hebrews says that your duty is to watch over your wrestlers as leaders who must give an account—and notice who you give that account to. If you were a high-school wrestling coach, you would answer to a school board. If you coached a professional sports team, you would be accountable to a general manager or owner. But spiritual wrestling coaches are accountable to an even higher authority—the Lord! Therefore, take your work very seriously.

If you're not a spiritual coach yet, remember that someday you very well could be. It's not as incredible as it may seem. What it takes is a willingness to share what God teaches you, and shows you, and does in your life, with others. The apostle Paul said that he and his companions would comfort others with the comfort they had received from God (2 Corinthians 1:3–6). That's the secret to being a successful coach. You don't need to be a Bible college or seminary graduate. You just need to pass along what God gives you.

> If you're not a spiritual coach yet, remember that someday you very well could be.

May God bless you, strengthen you, and stretch you as you wrestle with him one-on-one and as part of a team!

It's Your Turn!

Here are some questions to stimulate your own thoughts as you interact with this chapter, either by yourself or in a group.

1. Think of some Christians you'd like to have on your tag team. Are you honest enough with them for that to be possible? How could you be more honest with them and engage them in your bouts? Are there ever any bouts that shouldn't be shared with others?

2. What effect would it have on your actions and attitudes if you embraced the idea that "I belong to Christian groups in order that I might benefit others?"

3. Who are your coaches in the Christian faith right now? How, practically speaking, can you respect and obey them? Do you need even more coaches? How can you go about getting them?

4. Is it ever right to drop a coach? When and under what circumstances? How should the whole thing be handled?

5. Why do we tend to be self-centered? How can we become more "other directed"?

6. Are there any questions or concerns you have after reading this chapter?

7. Are there any questions or concerns you have after reading this book? What are some of the things you've learned? Has the book been helpful to you? Why or why not?

Leader's Guide

If you have decided (or have been drafted) to lead a group centered around this book, I have got good news for you, because the first thing I want you to do is *relax*! That's right. Relax! You don't have to suddenly become an expert on the material. You don't even have to prepare formal lessons. After all, you're tired enough from all that wrestling, aren't you? Oh, you can read a commentary or two on the Bible verses in a given chapter to glean a few tidbits to bring to the group if you want to. But you don't have to. In fact, your purpose is not to be a teacher, but to be a discussion leader.

Here are some suggestions on how to do that:

1. Remember that the reason the group exists is so that members can have a place to discuss their experiences with wrestling with God, their spiritual journeys, and their ideas and beliefs. As long as that happens, the meeting is a success. Therefore, don't get flustered if the group spends all of its time on question #3 and never gets to the rest of the questions in a given chapter. If a good discussion is taking place, that's all that matters. You can choose to visit the other questions during your next session, or just skip them all and move on, depending on the will of the group. But under no circumstances should you feel obligated to cover all the material each time.

2. If a question doesn't hit home for your group and doesn't elicit any responses, then just ask the next question.

3. Make sure that you come to the group prepared to be honest and open yourself. While the group isn't there to listen to you talk, you can model for them how to share. If you're not willing to open up, don't expect anyone else to either.

4. Don't look for "right answers" from members of the group, and certainly don't pressure, lecture, or correct them. For most of the questions there are no right answers. They are designed to get us to examine ourselves in light of the Bible and to allow God to interact with us as we do so. Therefore, there may be as many different answers to a question as there are people in a room.

5. Make sure everyone who wants to do so gets a chance to say something, but don't put anyone on the spot. If there's a lull in the conversation, say, "Does anyone else have any thoughts about the matter?" If one person is dominating the discussion, say, "You've made some good points and have gotten us thinking. Anyone else want to jump in here?" If it seems through body language or other cues that someone may be waiting to contribute, just say, "It seems as if you want to say something. Am I right?" If the answer is "No," just move on. But never say to a member, "You've been awfully quiet tonight. Why don't you answer the next question?" That embarrasses and puts the pressure on. It leads to people clamming up and skipping meetings. And who knows? Maybe God is working in silence within that person's heart.

And here are a few additional tips about discussion groups:

1. Set a time limit for the discussion—forty-five, sixty, or ninety minutes. People are more apt to commit to a group if they know the meetings won't drag on forever.

2. Seat the members of the group, including yourself, in a circle facing one another, whether it be in someone's living room, or around a table, or on chairs in the church's fellowship hall, or wherever. Do not stand and face the group as though you were giving a speech, or allow some members to sit in back of others. Remember, your purpose is to promote a discussion. People need to see and hear one another for that to take place.

3. Urge the members to read the chapters and think about the questions in advance. You will get more out of your time together that way. But don't worry. I know how busy people are, and that people forget to do assignments. So, many questions are designed to be able to be answered "cold" and "off-the-top-of-the-head." It just might not be as satisfying an experience for everyone, that's all.

4. Refreshments help! People are used to chatting over coffee or having lunch meetings. And goodies, or the promise of them later, can contribute to a spirit of friendliness and well-being that aids people in opening up during the discussion times.

5. If you have questions about leading your group or dealing with any problems that arise, contact your pastor or someone in the church who is known to be an experienced leader. There's no shame in asking for help!

6. Speaking of that, begin and end each session in prayer. After all, if God isn't in your meeting, what's the point of having it?

Now, ponder, grow, laugh, agonize, sympathize, and wrestle together. And may God bless you as you do.

We want to hear from you. Please send your comments about this book to us in care of zreview@zondervan.com. Thank you.

GRAND RAPIDS, MICHIGAN 49530 USA

WWW.ZONDERVAN.COM